— *the* —

SMART TRAVELER'S

PASSPORT

— *the* —

SMART TRAVELER'S

PASSPORT

399 TIPS *from*

SEASONED TRAVELERS

by the readers of
BUDGET TRAVEL

With an introduction by
NINA WILLDORF, Editor in Chief

Library of Congress Cataloging in Publication Number: 2006934225

ISBN: 978-1-59474-177-7

Printed in China

Typeset in Bembo, Helvetica, OCRA, OCRB, and Trade Gothic

Designed by Doogie Horner
Production management by Chris Veneziale

Distributed in North America by Chronicle Books
680 Second Street
San Francisco, CA 94107

10 9 8 7 6 5

Quirk Books
215 Church Street
Philadelphia, PA 19106
www.quirkbooks.com

CONTENTS < < < < < < < < < < < < < < <

Introduction

A good travel tip stands the test of time. As has this, our collection of 399 of the best tips we at *Budget Travel* magazine have received from our readers. We originally published this book two years ago, and not only is it still relevant, but the money saving ideas you'll find inside (all 133 of them!) are more useful than ever.

The savings tips you'll find in these pages are sometimes so simple they seem obvious (bring a calculator to a foreign market); other times they're brilliant in their silliness (reuse flip-flops from the nail salon as shower shoes). But taken together, they're simply brilliant. They're also accurate. You can be sure we've checked every last one to make sure they all hold up.

We're not quite done collecting tips yet. No doubt, there are countless more ways to make travel easier, faster, more affordable, and more fun. We're just waiting for you to tell us your secrets.

So send us your best at tips@budgettravel.com. If we run one in the magazine, we'll give you a free subscription. Now how's that for saving some money?

NINA WILLDORF
Editor in Chief
Budget Travel Magazine

CHAPTER ONE

<BT<<<<<<<<<<<<<<<<<<<<<<<<<<<<
9781594741777<<<<<<<<<<<<<<<<07

SPLURGING ACCOUNT When we come home at night, my wife and I each take a dollar from our wallets and put them in a special spot. We deposit what we've collected into a travel account at our bank every few months, so at the end of a year, we have $730 toward our next vacation—not counting interest.

Wayne Block, Seaford, Va.

THE NEXT FILES I've created files—some general (Southeast Asia), some specific (Hawaii)—for articles and clippings about places I'd like to visit in the future. I don't want all the good tips, restaurant recommendations, and out-of-the-ordinary itineraries to go to waste just because I'm not planning an immediate trip. The files don't have to be superorganized—just throw in the clippings, and you can weed through them later. You'll be glad you have the information when you do get a chance to go away.

Christine Size, Somerville, Mass.

BIG ON BROCHURES When planning a vacation, we send away for brochures from major tour operators. They provide hotel and restaurant recommendations and sightseeing itineraries, which we then duplicate on our own. Use this trick to mimic the vacation packages of high-end tour operators for what can turn out to be a fraction of the cost.

Raymond White, Dulles, Va.

IN-FLIGHT ADVISORS Ask your flight attendants for dining, lodging, shopping, and sightseeing advice. Most crews have up-to-the-minute information gleaned from layovers, which they're more than happy to share with passengers. You can count on flight attendants to seek out budget treasures. I know—I've been married to one for more than 21 years!

Fred Manget, Potomac Falls, Va.

NICHE READING Don't rely solely on guidebooks and travel magazines. Consulting specialty consumer magazines about art or food can also enhance a trip. Before heading off to Venice, we visited our local library and unearthed a food magazine that led us to trattorias, gelaterias, and wine bars enjoyed by locals that we probably would have missed otherwise. Similarly, a review in an art magazine allowed us to track down venues participating in the Venice Biennale, a huge international arts festival.

Sherel Purcell, Toronto, Ont.

SAILINGS ON SALE Some cruise lines offer discounts on a future sailing if you book it while on a current cruise. Back home, you can transfer the booking to your travel agent and work with them to try to lower the price even further. You'll be able to cancel your booking at no cost if you follow the cruise line's cancellation schedule. This is a great way to get some of your onboard expenses paid for in advance.

Jeff Pugel, New York, N.Y.

WEATHER OR NOT Check out worldclimate.com to find monthly average temperatures and rainfall for thousands of cities worldwide. You can avoid countries during their rainy seasons, and the information is useful for figuring out what to pack.

Elizabeth Bass, De Kalb, Ill.

RENT-A-CONCIERGE The help of a concierge at an expensive hotel is available even if you're staying at a motel across the street. Go to the concierge with $5 (or whatever the assistance is worth to you) held discreetly but visibly in your hand. Chances are you won't be asked whether you're staying at the hotel. This worked for us once when we were stranded by a blizzard. We tried to rebook our flights on our own, but phones at the airlines were busy for two days straight. The concierge at a fancy hotel a few blocks away got through on his first try and managed to rearrange our flights for us.

Janet Willer, Chicago, Ill.

SOUTH AMERICAN SAVINGS Planning a trip to South America? Join the nonprofit group South American Explorers (saexplorers.org) before you leave home. For $50, or $80 per couple, you'll get access to information on everything from volunteer opportunities to tour operators' deals, as well as a place to store luggage at offices in Quito, Lima, Buenos Aires, and Cuzco. Best of all, the discounts will easily cover the cost of membership. We were home free after the savings we received on our first reservation with an eco-lodge. The 10 percent we got off at our other hotels and some restaurants was gravy!

Molly Ogorzaly, Austin, Tex.

GOOGLING FOR DOLLARS Before traveling to any city, do a search on the Internet of the city name and the word "coupon" ("New Orleans coupon"). You will find many sites offering two-for-one, percentage-off, and dollar-off discounts. On a recent trip to St. Louis, we saved $100 at restaurants and attractions.

Carolyn J. Kubacki, Glendale Heights, Ill.

THAT'S ENTERTAINMENT If you wait to buy a discount-granting Entertainment Book until around six months before it expires (expiration is usually scheduled for November), you can often buy a $20 to $47 book for as little as $10, plus $5 shipping. Online access to the coupons is sold for $7 a month. These are great for vacations out of town.

Kitty Bennett, St. Petersburg, Fla.

DISCARDED DISCOUNTS Save major bucks by going onto eBay and purchasing coupons and gift certificates that others don't want or can't use for lodging, transportation, food, and admissions. I've found great discounts for airline and Amtrak tickets; car rentals; entrance to amusement parks such as SeaWorld, Disney, or Universal Studios; as well as overnights at many hotels. For example, I bought a $30 savings coupon at SeaWorld for only $1. Simply search for your destination and then type in "coupon" or "gift certificate."

Nathaniel V. Greenwood, Hummelstown, Pa.

CRUISE CONTROL < < < < < < < < < < < <

If your vacation spot is a major port of call for cruise ships, plan excursions for the days that the ships aren't docked. Tours will be less crowded, and you'll get to see and do a lot more.

Krista Fowles, New Haven, Conn.

GRAB MAG When we visit places we think we might return to, we collect copies of free tourist magazines. At home, we write the address of each magazine on a postcard. Six to eight weeks before our return visit, we send out the cards asking for a current copy. The magazines are full of useful information.

F. Richard Leininger, Schenectady, N.Y.

MAPS IN A SNAP For our road trip through the English countryside, I printed out a detailed map for every location we wanted to visit from multimap.com. I labeled each map with the day we planned on using it and wrote down the interesting sites and places to eat along the way. I kept them all in a folder and added brochures from the places we saw. It was a great souvenir upon returning home.

Karen Holt, Woodinville, Wash.

COUPON CENTRAL Destinationcoupons.com supplies free discount coupons for cities all over the United States and the world. Print them out on your home computer and save on hotels, shows, rental cars, restaurants, and many other activities.

Donald Bertolet, Holland, Pa.

LOW-FARE FINDER I teach a Tulane University seminar on independent European travel for first-timers. Until recently, I advocated Europe's great rail networks as the way to go. Now, with the plethora of budget airlines, I recommend a combination of the two. But it makes the planning stage—which I find almost as much fun as actually taking the trip—more involved. Thank goodness for whichbudget.com, a Web site that lists, by city, which budget airlines serve which cities. Then, to find links to all of Europe's state railway Web sites, visit railfaneurope.net. Each site generally features a travel planner and, almost invariably, an English-language option.

Brian Hughes, Crestview, Fla.

DULY NOTEBOOKED Love researching your destination online, but don't know how to organize all those printouts, maps, guidebooks, and tips? I get a 5 x 7" spiral notebook (Mead makes one with a sturdy cover and a pocket insert), a set of index tabs, and some glue. Divide the notebook into sections with the tabs (sights, maps, currency converter, restaurants, etc.). Photocopy—in reduction mode—all the info you want to bring, and glue it into the appropriate section. I leave plenty of pages for my journals. This creates an all-in-one personal guide that you can read again years after your trip!

Michele Graves, Tucson, Ariz.

NO PARKING If you're planning a driving tour of Italy, make Venice your first or last stop. You won't use your rental car in the city—you'll travel by boat or foot instead—and garages there charge upward of $30 a day.

Karen Kunz, Toms River, N.J.

FOLDER ALL Before leaving for a vacation, I print out all our reservations and directions, and I create a contact sheet for emergencies. Then I gather all the papers together, punch some holes, and place them in a folder that has a middle section for three-holed papers. The side pockets hold brochures, business cards, ticket stubs, receipts, and maps that we collect along the way and want to bring home for our scrapbook.

Sonal Gupte, Rockville, Md.

LOVE YOUR LAYOVER Long layovers are less painful if you escape the airport. On the way home from India, we found ourselves with a seven-hour layover in Mumbai. We took a ten-minute shuttle ride to the Leela Kempinski Mumbai hotel (theleela.com). After leaving our bags at the front desk we bought $11 day passes for the health club, which gave us access to the steam room, sauna, outdoor pool, and locker room. I booked a half-hour back massage for another $15. We had a glass of wine in the lobby bar and took the shuttle back to the airport. It was nice to relax and freshen up before the long flight home.

Kathleen Sutter, Manassas, Va.

DAYLIGHT SAVINGS <<<<<<<<<<<<

When you change your clocks back or forward, be sure to check the expiration date on all your frequent-flier miles. This way they're checked twice a year. We overlooked one of the many accounts in our household and lost a free ticket when the miles expired.

Lynda Self, Northport, Ala.

YE SHALL RECEIVE If you plan to book an excursion in New Zealand, call in advance and ask the tour operator if they're running any coupons in local magazines or newspapers. They'll generally tell you exactly where to find them, and you can save up to 50 percent. On one occasion, we couldn't find the actual coupon, but since we mentioned the ad, the company decided to give us a discount anyway!

Renee and Juan Gala, Indianapolis, Ind.

LONDON BRIDGE It's often cheaper to buy a ticket to London and then fly onward within Europe via a regional low-cost airline. Last summer, my husband and I bought consolidator tickets to London for $397. From there, we flew EasyJet to Nice for $72. The total cost was $469—much less than flying directly to Nice, plus we enjoyed a stopover in London.

Jasmine Tata, Antioch, Ill.

VOYAGE VETTING When I'm planning a trip, I almost always call the hotel concierge before I arrive—and if my hotel doesn't have one, I call a hotel that does. Recently, I asked for advice on what to see since I only had four days in a new city. I told the concierge what I thought I should try to do, and she said I had too many things packed into four days. She gave me a list of hot spots to visit and places to avoid, and even recommended a florist to call on for fresh flowers. With her help, my trip was far more enjoyable than it would have been otherwise.

Brian Berg, Cape Coral, Fla.

SHARE THE BURDEN Once we know where we're going, my girlfriends and I divide up the list of things we'd like to do on our trip and put someone in charge of each item on the list. Then that person does the legwork by finding directions and prices, making reservations (if necessary), and researching nearby places to stop for a snack or a meal. Our method means that no one person is doing all the planning.

Carol J. Leisch, Normal, Ill.

SOLO, SO LOW When looking for the lowest airfare, I've found that in some cases the best rates pop up when searching for one traveler instead of two. Recently, I wanted to buy one-way tickets from New York to Orlando for two people and came up with $87 per person. But when I selected one traveler, the fare dropped to $72.

Yoshi Matsuda, Tigard, Ore.

EARLY BIRDS Try to book the first flight out in the morning, because those planes often arrive at the airport the evening before. You won't have to rely on an incoming plane, which could be delayed or canceled due to bad weather elsewhere, resulting in your own flight being delayed or canceled.

George Glover, Brunswick, Maine

MAXIMIZING MILES Using your frequent-flier miles, you might be able to visit two cities on one ticket. For example, my wife and I always trade in our Delta miles when we visit our daughters in Dallas and San Francisco. Because we have to fly through Dallas to get to San Francisco on Delta, we can stop over in Dallas for as long as we want before continuing on to San Francisco—and we use only one frequent-flier ticket each.

Harry Bishop, Charleston, S.C.

PRICE PACKAGES OUT Though they're often the best deals around, don't assume that packaged vacations always offer the biggest bang for your buck. My wife and I were ready to book an air/hotel package to Maui when we noticed a sale on Aloha Airlines ($280 round trip from Oakland). I added up the total cost of the trip if purchased separately and saved $400 over comparable packages from various tour operators. We used the extra money to stay in a nicer hotel and to rent a convertible!

Kleem Chaudhary, Hayward, Calif.

BIDDING WAR Play *Let's Make a Deal* when you're shopping for vacations at travel shows or expos. Go armed with your own research and a credit card. (You're likely to get a better price if you know what the vacation is worth, and if you're willing to buy it on the spot.) I picked two Caribbean cruises and headed to the *New York Times* Travel Show. After haggling with the competing cruise lines, I was offered the first cruise for $50 less than the best price I'd found online, and they threw in free trip insurance. In the end, I chose the second—$30 off with a free upgrade to a balcony stateroom—and truly got a bargain.

Michael Marcarello, South Salem, N.Y.

READ 'EM AND REAP Pay close attention to those newsletters enclosed in your frequent-flier statements. They usually contain special offers and promotions that can earn you double or triple miles if you stay at a certain hotel or eat at a certain restaurant.

Kim Borisenko, Boston, Mass.

COOKIE MONSTER I used a well-known travel site to price tickets for a trip to Las Vegas. The flight I wanted was available, but I decided to wait to see if prices would come down. That flight stopped being listed after a week, and the next best flight kept getting more expensive. About five weeks later, I checked prices from a different PC. Whaddya know? The original flight was available, for $50 less than that next-best flight. That same evening I checked again from my PC. The flight I wanted was not available, so I deleted the cookies for the site and tried again. Voilà! The flight I wanted at the price I wanted. Moral of the story: Clean up your cookies—it could save you money!

Kelly Malasics, Bridgeport, Conn.

TRIP ADVISOR To find the perfect destination with airfare that meets your budget, try Travelocity's Dream Maps travel tool (travelocity.com). Select a maximum fare and a type of destination—city, national park, etc.—and the Web site will display a variety of trips matching that description.

Matt Vance, Austin, Tex.

SPLITTING THE BILL If you don't have enough frequent-flier miles to get to Europe, use your miles to reach a major airport in the United States and then pay for the overseas flight from there. For a trip to Ireland, my husband and I used Delta SkyMiles to get from Cincinnati to New York's JFK airport and from there took Aer Lingus to Ireland. The Aer Lingus Internet special was $267 per person. A Delta flight from Cincinnati to Ireland was $1,150 for two. We saved more than $600.

Kristin Farrell, Surrey, UK

PAPER TRAIL If you book a package over the Internet, print out all the details of what's included and take it with you. When a hotel desk clerk in Paris said that the breakfast buffet we had enjoyed for the previous seven mornings was not included in our package, I was able to show him the printouts and prove him wrong. He apologized profusely and wiped the breakfast charges from our bill.

John Lavelle, Avon Lake, Ohio

IS THE PRICE RIGHT? Before using frequent-flier miles, investigate how much the flight actually costs. For example, it takes at least 25,000 miles per person to travel from Boston to Alaska. The same flight cost us $288. After paying for our tickets, we received enough additional miles to travel for free to Sweden instead of Alaska!

Bobby Pellant, Waltham, Mass.

PRICELINE PARAMETERS Priceline was a total pig in a poke for me, so I never used the Web site—until I found out about biddingfortravel.com. This helpful Web site gives potential bidders an idea of prices that are being accepted (and declined) on priceline.com for particular dates and properties (or airfares or car rentals). I got the Hyatt Regency Miami for $35 per night because of this!

C. Sue Mecham, Challis, Idaho

PACKAGES UNPACKAGED When seeking a cheap airfare, don't forget to consult the Web sites of the major charter tour operators—like Apple Vacations, TNT Vacations, Vacation Express, or SunTrips—which frequently sell air-only tickets in addition to air-and-hotel packages. Doing so helped me slash the cost of round-trip airfare to visit my mother in Las Vegas by well over 50 percent.

Pam McMenamin, Louisville, Colo.

GET A CHARGE Before booking your next ski trip or reserving a table for dinner, find out what your credit card company has to offer. American Express sometimes has discounts on lift tickets; MasterCard has offered buy-one-get-one-free at local restaurants; and Discover Card has access to deals to Universal Studios. Check out americanexpress.com/offerzone, mastercard.com (be sure to click on Promotions), and discovercard.com.

Connie A. Yu, New York, N.Y.

INFREQUENT FLIER? Preserve even the small number of frequent-flier miles you may obtain by making occasional use of a particular carrier; the miles can be worth money. Even if you don't regularly fly on Delta, Northwest, Continental, or several other airlines, sign up for their frequent-flier programs when you book a long or overseas flight. Points.com allows you to redeem miles for magazine subscriptions, music downloads, and other products. You can also use miles to get small discounts on purchases at retailers such as Amazon.com.

Jonelle Niffenegger, Evanston, Ill.

FOREIGN EXCHANGE I was booking tickets online for an upcoming flight to Europe from the East Coast. One particularly attractive fare was offered on a U.S. airline as well as on its foreign "partner airline." Same plane, same flight, same base price. But it was more than $100 cheaper per ticket to book with the foreign airline versus the U.S. one. We saved more than $400 for four tickets, but we'll be on the same plane!

Lori Uhl, Glenville, Pa.

SINGAPORE GALORE < < < < < < < < < < <

The last time I had a layover in Singapore, I took advantage of one of the free tours offered from the airport—a harbor cruise. The tours are available to passengers with layovers of five hours or more. Look for the Free Singapore Tour counters on the second levels of terminals 1 and 2.

Marcia Mac Dougall, South Gate, Calif.

SAME-DAY SAVIOR Many tourist-information offices provide discounted same-day booking services for local lodgings. My husband and I discovered this when we accidentally left a midweek gap in our travel plans between my husband's conference hotel and our B&B in Charleston. Instead of adding another night at either location, we stayed at one of the more elegant inns (normally over $200) for $70, courtesy of the Charleston Convention and Visitors Bureau.

Audrey E. Vance, Bonita Springs, Fla.

ELIMINATE THE MIDDLEMAN Cruise lines offer packaged side trips at their ports of call. If you go online and look for these expeditions ahead of time, you can book directly with the tour companies and save money.

Cindy Rucker, Jekyll Island, Ga.

CANCELLATION VALIDATION If you make a hotel reservation online and then cancel online, print out and save the cancellation confirmation for at least two billing cycles past your trip. After our vacation, I found a "no-show" charge on my credit card for a room that I'd canceled well in advance. Without the confirmation, I had no way to contest the bill.

Karen Griffith-Hedberg, Eugene, Ore.

REPEAT THE QUESTION Don't settle for the first answer to your travel question. If you need flight information, it's a good idea to phone the airline more than once and ask the same question. Recently, I wanted to see if I could fly standby on an earlier flight the same day. The first time I called, I was told that the earlier flight was booked. The second time, however, an agent said there were in fact seats available, and I could certainly fly standby. In the end, not only was I able to get on the flight, but I was upgraded to first class.

Lynn Babcock, Dexter, Mich.

DIVIDE AND CONQUER We've noticed that when booking a flight for our family under one reservation, some airlines will only credit the 1,500 bonus miles (500 for booking online, 500 each way for printing boarding passes) to the person whose name the reservation is under. This is regardless of whether the other family members have mileage accounts. To avoid this, make a separate reservation for each of your family members and then pick seats together.

Martin Vasquez, Patterson, N.Y.

KEEP SHOPPING AROUND Check fares periodically after booking your airfare. The airline may have a sale, and buying new tickets could save you money—even after you pay the change penalty. My wife and I used Travelocity's Fare Finder to pocket $187 each on a recent trip from Seattle to New York City, simply by reticketing.

Doug Rittenhouse, Port Angeles, Wash.

PEOPLE POWER After I was unable to locate any awards seats online for a wide selection of days and routes, I called the airline. An agent told me that the airline's Web site isn't allowed to book awards seats for its partner airlines, but agents can. Within minutes, I had enough options that I found it difficult to make a decision.

Carol Muth, Raleigh, N.C.

DON'T MISS THE BOAT Here's an important tip for cruising in winter: Fly into the port a day or two before your ship is scheduled to depart. We booked a Costa Rican cruise but were stuck in New York, where all flights out of JFK airport were canceled. Itineraries that include stops in places with airports can allow people to catch up. Ours didn't.

Anne Schweisguth, Swiftwater, Pa.

CHAPTER TWO

BEFORE YOU GO

★(36-77)★

PACKING CAREFULLY

AND PREPARING TO LEAVE

IMMIGRATION 20YCBB

<BT<<<<<<<<<<<<<<<<<<<<<<<<<<<
9781594741777<<<<<<<<<<<<<<<07

SPLIT UP YOUR STUFF If you're traveling with a companion, pack half of your belongings in his or her suitcase and vice versa. This way, if one piece of luggage gets lost, you'll each still have some clothing.

Christina Costigan, Pawtucket, R.I.

PROTECTIVE FILM To ensure the studs of pierced and delicate earrings don't get damaged, I put them in a film canister. An added benefit is that they're less likely to be stolen when left in a suitcase or hotel room, because thieves presume there's nothing inside but film.

Alison Taylor Fastov, Washington, D.C.

BATTERY SWITCHEROO I reverse the batteries in my portable CD player before packing it in my suitcase or backpack, in case it's accidentally turned on when my bag is jostled. I came up with the idea after arriving at my destination to find that the brand-new batteries I'd put into my Walkman were dead.

Chris Giaimo, New York, N.Y.

KNOW YOUR LIMITS Pack light, or that great deal you found on airfare won't seem that great. On a Ryanair flight between Glasgow and Dublin, my husband and I were charged over $100 for excess baggage weight (the airline tickets themselves cost less than half that). Be sure to check the weight limits—especially on low-fare airlines—before you leave home.

Lynne Heath, Hudson, N.H.

THE TOTAL TOTE The best carry-on bag that I've found is a gardener's tote. It has lots of pockets on the outside and room inside for a medium-size purse, yet it's small enough to sit comfortably at my feet on a bus or plane.

Sheila Monk, Richland, Mo.

TWO TONES OF FUN Pick just two colors to mix and match throughout your trip. You'll cut down on luggage, not least because you won't have to bring a bunch of shoes to match a wide assortment of colors.

Lori Fields, Salisbury, Md.

DOUBLE DUTY To save space, pack items for travel that you can use in at least two ways. In a pinch, shampoo can double for detergent when washing your clothes (carry the bottle in a Ziploc bag in your suitcase); sandals or flip-flops also function as slippers; and a swimsuit cover-up can serve as a bathrobe.

Patricia LaRock, Woodstock, Minn.

BOUNCE OF PREVENTION Place a fabric softener sheet in your suitcase when packing. It'll absorb odors and dampness and keep clothing smelling fresh. It's most beneficial in warm, humid climates and while at sea. I found this quite useful during my twenty-three years in the U.S. Navy.

Edward Jewell, Washington, D.C.

HIP TO BE SQUARE Avoid spills in your Dopp kit. Cut up plastic grocery bags into little squares and place them under the tops of toiletries to prevent leaks. Discard the squares upon arrival, but bring extras for the trip back.

Roland Zuniga, Richardson, Tex.

DUCT TAPE DISPENSER Everyone knows that duct tape is great for helping out in travel emergencies, but no one wants to lug around a bulky roll of the stuff. By wrapping a few feet onto a pencil or ballpoint pen, you'll get a miniature roll that does not take up much in the way of additional space.

Randy Hartselle, Lincoln, Calif.

GEAR SHIFT My husband and I are retired, and we take two trips abroad each year. When unpacking, I put items we use repeatedly on each trip (flashlight, alarm clock, travel-size toiletries, etc.) into a box and keep it stored near the suitcases. No more searching or trying to remember if I've got everything for the next journey—it's all in one place.

Mary Meikle, Whitewater, Wis.

REPURPOSED POUCHES I started saving the heavy-duty plastic wrappers that sheets and curtains come in. Most have zippers or snaps—great to hold everything from toiletries to shoes to wet swimsuits. And I bet airport security must love them because they're see-through.

Terry Schmieder, Attica, N.Y.

PAPER PLASTIC Recycle the long plastic bags in which you receive your home-delivered newspapers. Slip your shoes into the bags before packing them in your suitcase.

Robert E. Jones, Fairhope, Ala.

NALGENIUS! Instead of packing a complete shaving kit, my husband fills his wide-mouth Nalgene water bottle with items such as razors, spare contact lenses, eyeglasses, toothbrush, and so on. This turned out to be particularly useful on our trip to Costa Rica, where we also took the bottle on our day hikes to volcanoes and the jungle.

Terry Clemson, Plymouth Meeting, Pa.

WAX FIX If the zipper on your luggage or your clothing is giving you any trouble, rubbing some lip balm or candle wax onto the teeth should loosen it.

Marko Anderson, Huntington Beach, Calif.

ON SPECS Use the shoe-shine mitt often found in hotel bathrooms to store your sunglasses. They fit nicely inside the pouch, and when you take them out, you have a soft material to clean them with. For extra protection while traveling, I store my sunglasses inside the shoe-shine mitt, fold the end closed, and then place it in my glasses case.

Dan Coviello, Suffern, N.Y.

DIVIDE DIRTY DUDS Take along an extra duffel bag for your laundry. As your vacation progresses, throw dirty clothes into the duffel, keeping your suitcase for fresh clothes. At the end of the trip, put a tag on the bag and check it at the airport. This will also give you space in your luggage to bring home souvenirs or new clothes.

Susan Wiley, St. Petersburg, Fla.

OVERNIGHT CASE An extra contact lens case holds enough toiletries for a short trip. Squeeze a few dabs of toothpaste into one side and perhaps some facial cleanser or moisturizer in the other side. Just the right amount of each will fit for your overnights or weekends away.

Jen Shoemaker, Bozeman, Mont.

Q-TIP TIP My husband packs Q-tips in a plastic cassette case. It's small and snaps shut, keeping the cotton swabs clean and dry.

Nancy Bastian, Brewster, N.Y.

NO THERMOS NECESSARY After looking for years for the perfect toiletries bag and being frustrated by many that were less than ideal, I finally discovered one that is just right: a soft-sided lunch box I bought at the supermarket. It has an outer zipped pocket with small compartments and slots perfect for often-used items like a toothbrush and toothpaste. There's a small removable zipper pouch inside (meant for a small ice pack) for those smaller, hard-to-find items like nail files and pill bottles. The remaining space inside is just right for larger items like shampoo and hand lotion. Other helpful features include both a small handle and shoulder strap and a waterproof, easy-to-clean interior. As an elementary school teacher, I know firsthand that it'll last: It was designed to withstand daily use by kids!

Jennifer Minton, Glencoe, Calif.

SOAP? NOPE Travel soap dishes—the colorful plastic ones that have hinged lids—stop small, fragile items from getting damaged or lost in your bags. I can easily label and use them again and again and again.

Revon Wolf, Culver City, Calif.

WATERPROOF YOUR BAG On a trip to Molokai, the plane we were on was small, and luggage was crammed in every which way. At baggage claim, we noticed that someone had packed a bottle of Pine-Sol, and it had broken and leaked everywhere. Now we line our suitcases with garbage bags to protect our clothes—just in case. (It's also smart in case your bag gets left on the tarmac in a downpour.)

Aaron Lisle, Sioux City, Iowa

SCENT PROTECTION Put your perfume and cologne bottles inside pairs of rolled-up socks to keep them cushioned during your journey.

Joia Starks, Union City, N.J.

HAVE YOU SEEN THIS SUITCASE? In order to provide any reimbursement for a lost suitcase, most airlines and insurance companies require an itemized list of exactly what was inside it. Unfortunately, remembering everything you packed after the fact is virtually impossible. To avoid the headache, take pictures of the items you're going to put in your suitcase with your digital camera or cell phone. The photos will make creating the list a breeze, and, in the event of a dispute with the airline or insurance agent, you have some visual evidence of ownership.

Erica Rounsefell, Mesa, Ariz.

A-LIST < < < < < < < < < < < < < < < <

It's unnecessary to make a packing list for each trip. Instead, draw up a master list with everything you might need on any given trip—from ski goggles to snorkels, slippers to saline solution. Save it on your computer. Before you start packing, cross out anything you don't need for that particular trip.

Bonnie Herbst, Ventura, Calif.

PILLS WITHOUT SPILLS My husband cut an old contact lens case in two and uses the halves to carry his medication when we're traveling. He prefers them to regular pillboxes because lens cases are watertight and compact enough to carry inside a shirt pocket.

Jean Holtmann, Broken Arrow, Okla.

PULLING A FAST ONE I try to avoid checking any luggage, but the airlines are getting stricter every day about the size and weight of carry-ons. So when I pack, I put any important stuff in a plastic bag and place it in a front pocket. If I'm told to check my carry-on when I get to the gate, I can just pull out the smaller bag and board.

Alena Kerins, Stamford, Conn.

REFILL AND REUSE Once the hotel shampoo bottles I always seem to bring home are empty, I refill them with my own brand of shampoo, conditioner, and shower gel—instead of buying travel-size containers at the drugstore. I toss them, along with other small items (toothbrush, toothpaste, nail file, pillboxes, and a comb), into a medium-size Ziploc bag, and I'm ready to go; the clear plastic lets me find things easily.

Donna Cover, Sharon, Mass.

TWO IS BETTER THAN ONE When I travel for business, I usually tack on a few extra days to do something active like hike in a nearby national park. I find that by taking two small suitcases instead of a single large one, I stay better organized and less burdened. I keep my business clothes, papers, and laptop in one bag and hiking clothes and gear in another. I leave the suitcase I'm not using at the time in the rental car and easily carry the lightweight case with the equipment and clothes I need into my hotel.

Ellen Worthing, Baltimore, Md.

ZIPPER ZEST No longer do the many key chains I get as advertising languish in bureau drawers. I attach one or two at the ends of my luggage zippers. They make it easier to work the zippers and help me identify my luggage on airport carousels.

Marie J. Kilker, Sarasota, Fla.

SUPER SLIPPERS My husband and I keep the stretchy slipper-socks that some airlines provide. (We've gotten them on Virgin Atlantic in economy class and on almost all airlines in business class.) They're great to use when packing shoes: Just slip each shoe into a sock, and you'll prevent clothes from getting marked up by the soles. As a bonus, you'll have slippers to wear when you're away from home. The socks are machine-washable and can last for many years.

Wendy Barr, St. Helena Island, S.C.

PLASTIC FANTASTIC Dry-cleaning bags stop clothes from wrinkling. Slide each garment into its own bag (leave the hanger at home) and place them flat on your bed, one on top of another. Then carefully fold the entire stack to fit it in your suitcase. Once you get to your hotel, hang everything up as soon as you can. You'll never unpack a suitcase of wrinkled clothes again.

Claudette Christman, Colonial Heights, Va.

DIVVY DO When I travel with friends, we decide ahead of time who's going to bring what. If we're sharing a suite or have adjoining rooms, we don't need multiple hair dryers and umpteen bottles of shampoo. With the weight limits on baggage, we'll need the extra space in our suitcases for souvenirs!

Haley Christensen, Henderson, Nev.

QUARTER IMPOUNDER Use an empty M&M's Minis tube to carry quarters. The top holds tightly, but still pops open easily enough, and the size is perfect to slip into a car door or bag. I find it very useful when traveling by car (for tolls and parking meters) and by airplane (for luggage carts or newspapers).

Judi McDowell, Aiea, Hawaii

ULTIMATE FRISBEE I like to bring a Frisbee when I travel. At the hotel, it's a convenient place to collect car keys, loose change, my ChapStick, and any other small objects I normally keep in my pockets. I always know where everything is, and things won't fall off the nightstand. It's also handy to have so you can play Frisbee at a nearby park or beach.

Margot Johnson, Irvine, Calif.

PUTTING ON THE SPRITZ I used to lug around a clothes steamer and adapter to stay wrinkle-free while on the road, but I've since opted for something more low-tech. I now travel with a Platypus collapsible bottle and a spray bottle head. After checking into my hotel, I immediately hang my clothes and give them a spritz with water from the spray bottle. After several hours, the wrinkles fall out, and the clothing is dry and ready to wear.

Dr. Cornelia Cho, Marietta, Ga.

SOUND ADVICE During a visit to Mexico City, I was sitting in a plaza near a fountain, watching the locals stroll around in their Sunday best. Nearby, an older gentleman was playing a concertina; his music perfectly framed the scene. I took lots of pictures, but I didn't have a way to capture that music. Now I pack a small tape recorder along with my camera.

Kieran Sala, Pasadena, Calif.

GOOD VIBRATIONS My hearing loss once made it impossible to hear any alarm clock. Then I found the Shake Awake, an alarm clock that vibrates. I no longer stare at the ceiling all night prior to an early flight in fear of oversleeping. I clip Shake Awake to my pillow or place it on a hard surface near my bed, where its rattling definitely gets my attention.

Kathy Hopkins, Jackson, N.J.

LIGHT READING I always pack a Petzl Tikka Plus headlamp. It's small, weighs next to nothing, and is perfect for reading in bed at night without disturbing my husband. They're sold online and at outdoor-gear stores for about $33.

Linda Smejkal, Hazelhurst, Wis.

CHARGE IT! Batteries for cameras, laptops, cell phones, and other devices can be charged at night in your hotel room. But if you're doing a lot of driving, you might want to buy an inverter to charge them while on the road. Inverters (which plug into the car's cigarette lighter) are small, inexpensive, and can be purchased at auto-supply, variety, or electronics stores.

Kay Euhus, Springfield, Ore.

POSTER PROTECTOR I travel with a mailing tube in my suitcase because I often buy paintings, drawings, and maps. My souvenirs always arrive home safe and sound. I just leave the mailing tube in my suitcase until the next trip.

Abbie-Stuart Fox, Durham, N.C.

SARONG IT'S RIGHT Lightweight, washable, and multifunctional, a cotton sarong is an easy and practical addition to every traveler's don't-leave-home-without-it bag! I've used mine as a swimsuit cover-up, as a picnic blanket on the grounds of a château in the Loire Valley, as a temporary skirt (over my shorts) in a Bangkok temple, and as an extra pillow while hiking the South Rim of the Grand Canyon. It's also handy as an airplane blanket, emergency towel, or tablecloth.

Nicole Serafica, Langhorne, Pa.

INSTANT AMBIENCE I always pack several tea lights, a small vial of essential oils, and matches. Tea lights, when placed in a water glass for extra safety, banish stale or unpleasant smells in hotel rooms. The essential oils work wonders when a drop is placed on a warm lightbulb.

Stephanie Hartselle, Chicago, Ill.

GET IN GEAR When you travel to a beach destination, bring your own snorkel gear. We bought snorkels, masks, and fins at home for half-off (at an end-of-summer sale) before a trip to Hawaii. They didn't take up much room in our luggage, and we would have spent as much or more renting the equipment.

Keely McNerney, Alexandria, Va.

RECEIPTS IN A ROW If you have to save receipts while traveling, purchase a plastic coupon holder to help you keep track of them (it'll also protect them). Label each section of the coupon holder by category (hotel, rental car, gas, food, etc.) or by day of the week. The coupon holders are compact and easily fit into a laptop case, purse, or travel bag.

Ursalene Davis, Celina, Tex.

HEY, MISTER! During the hot months of summer, I plan to travel with a very small spray bottle. I'll fill it with water and use it as a mister to keep cool. I got this idea when we stayed at the Noga Hilton in Cannes. On the dresser was a pink aerosol can full of Evian water. I took it with us sightseeing and, wow, it was so refreshing to spritz water on our faces.

Joy Shebroe, Walnut, Calif.

STAIN FIGHTER Shout Wipes take up very little space in your purse or backpack and are invaluable for treating stains. While traveling on an airplane, I gave one to a most grateful Italian after he spilled wine on his tie. Our friendship extended through customs, and we're now e-mail pals. Great stuff!

Marilyn Rogers, Iowa City, Iowa

BAD-WEATHER FRIEND Put a few plastic trash bags in the outer pockets of your suitcases and carry-ons. If you arrive at your destination and it's raining, you can cover your luggage with the bags while you make your way to your hotel. Just cut a slit for handles or straps.

Barbara Gesse, Greensboro, N.C.

GOOD SHIP When my husband and I travel with our children, our luggage is weighed down by diapers, formula, and other necessities. To save space and hassle, we now ship ahead most of those items to our hotel. We also came across a Web site called babiestravellite.com, where we can order supplies and have them shipped anywhere in the world.

Mina Camera, San Gabriel, Calif.

BUTTON YOUR CLIP < < < < < < < < < <

Attach a few carabiners—the kind of clips rock climbers use—to the top of your wheeled suitcase. Purses, cameras, and shopping bags can be clipped to your suitcase, giving your hands and shoulders a rest while you're walking around the airport.

Kathryn Murphy, Satellite Beach, Fla.

DISPOSABLE BATH MAT Paper place mats can be useful anywhere there's an outdoor shower. By stepping onto a place mat after a bush shower in Botswana, I managed to keep my feet clean and avoided getting dirt in my clothes.

Sandy S. Hogan, Las Vegas, Nev.

BABY YOURSELF Baby wipes aren't just for babies. Slip a travel-size pack into your carry-on bag and use the wipes to kill germs on public toilet seats and in phone booths. In a pinch, they can also remove stubborn stains from clothing.

Farrah Farhang, Fremont, Calif.

BUNGEE FUN Bungee cords make versatile travel accessories. They come in handy at the airport for lashing a duffel bag to a wheeled suitcase. They can be hooked together and used as a clothesline for swimsuits, towels, etc. On skiing trips, hook them onto ski boots to create carrying handles. While camping, use them to secure tarps, to suspend a lantern from a nearby tree limb, or to secure items in a canoe. They even hold your pants up if you misplace your belt.

Keith Saul, Kokomo, Ind.

DELICATE SITUATION Instead of bringing one of those bungee cables to hang-dry my delicates and socks, I pack a couple of mini plastic hangers—the ones that bras and panties come on when you buy them. They take up very little room in my luggage and can be thrown away at the end of the trip.

Monica Pileggi, Frederick, Md.

WHAT'S SHAKING? Pack a travel-size shampoo container refilled with detergent and a one-gallon Ziploc bag for when you need to wash hosiery, bras, and other delicate undergarments. Put a few drops of detergent into the bag and fill it part way with water. Place the garment in the bag, close it up, and shake it around for a few minutes. Instant washing machine! For larger pieces of clothing, I've used the plastic laundry bags supplied at most hotels. Just hold on to the open end tightly.

Erika Kumada, Marina del Rey, Calif.

WHEN CHEATERS PROSPER When overseas, I carry a "cheat sheet" that includes exchange rates and metric conversions. Currency conversions are available at oanda.com.

Carol Vela, Denton, Tex.

INFO IN A FLASH I use an inexpensive, thumb-size USB flash drive to store medical and insurance contacts, confirmation codes, credit card numbers, addresses, and phone numbers. It fits in a secure zip pocket in my travel purse. If I don't have my laptop, I can insert the flash drive in most hotel or Internet café computers. Some USB flash drives password-protect your data, or you can download a free encryption program.

Linda Steven, Saint Paul, Minn.

JOURNAL IN A JIFFY Pack a glue stick for journaling. Rather than bringing home an envelope full of ticket stubs and mementos, you can glue them into your journal as you're traveling. You'll have a better chance of remembering what the ticket was for if you label it right away.

Jon Chun, San Jose, Calif.

PUT A DAMPER ON IT Before I embark on a trip, I cover the dirt of my potted plants with plastic bags after watering them well. (Cut a few slits in the bags and keep plants out of direct sunlight.) The soil will stay damp for about three weeks.

Jean Walsh, Thiensville, Wis.

WITH A TWIST Carry a twist tie in your wallet. Among other ingenious uses, a twist tie can temporarily replace a lost screw on a pair of glasses. Just peel the paper or plastic off the tie so you have bare wire, insert it where the screw once was, and twist to tighten. Unlike Scotch tape or a safety pin, a twist tie is small enough to remain hidden and strong enough to hold until you're able to replace the screw.

Suzanne Prendergast, Chicago, Ill.

FLOSS LEADER <<<<<<<<<<<<<

I never leave home without dental floss. I've used it as a clothesline between tents in Botswana's Okavango Delta and to replace a lost screw for my sunglasses in Malaysia. I even cut off a piece of floss the size of my waist and headed to the night markets in Bangkok. My "tape measure" assured a perfect fit!

Kristi Hemmer, Cordova, Tenn.

SHEETS ARE NEAT Bring your own linens. They're useful in a million different ways. Obviously a soft cotton pillowcase makes those scratchy airplane pillows bearable, but it can also be used to gather loose items when deplaning. A nice sheet will cover up an ugly bedspread or sofa, and makes a great tablecloth or picnic blanket.

Dori Egan, Pleasant Hill, Calif.

HOLD EVERYTHING Water-bottle holsters are good for more than holding water. I own several Water Bottle Totes by Outdoor Research (orgear.com). With their Velcro-like straps, I can fasten them anywhere—to my belt, camera strap, fanny pack, purse, or airplane seat. I've used them at various times to carry my camera, binoculars, snacks, umbrella, battery-powered fan, flashlight, sunglasses, a windbreaker, and a rain poncho.

Patricia S. Beagle, Williamsville, N.Y.

RECYCLED GLASSES Whenever my husband and I get new pairs of eyeglasses, we relegate the old ones to our luggage, along with an inexpensive repair kit from the drugstore. If something happens while we're away from home, we can hopefully fix the glasses ourselves. If they're beyond saving, we have the backup pairs to get us through the rest of the trip.

Carol Alabaster, Phoenix, Ariz.

ON THE HOOK Restrooms abroad rarely have hooks on stall doors. Our solution: Pack a small S hook in your shoulder bag and make use of a hole in the wall, a pipe, etc., to hang purses, jackets, or anything else you want to keep off the floor. S hooks can be found in most hardware stores, near the screws and bolts.

Arthur and Marcia Lloyd, Pocatello, Idaho

ACCESSORY ACCESS When I go on a trip that requires me to accessorize a number of outfits, I buy little Ziploc bags and place the appropriate jewelry/panty hose/scarf inside. Then I punch a hole just big enough to slide the bag over the outfit's hanger. This way, my panty hose stay snag-free and my jewelry never gets misplaced.

Gina Beyer, New York, N.Y.

CABLE LABELS Anyone traveling with multiple electronic devices (laptops, PDAs, cell phones, digital cameras, MP3 players) can easily confuse all the accessories that come with them. To keep all battery chargers, USB cables, media cards, and owner's manuals safe, dry, and organized, place them in individual Ziploc bags. You can put a label inside the bag to identify the contents, and one label wrapped around each cable to identify it.

Alyse Liebowitz, Holmdel, N.J.

OUTFIT INSIGHT If your children are old enough to dress themselves, consider this packing tip: Put each outfit (including socks and underwear) into a Ziploc bag and pack one bag for each day you'll be on vacation. It will save both time and aggravation, and may even prevent items from getting left behind.

Robert E. Jones, Fairhope, Ala.

THIS IS KEY Bring a single-hole punch and lanyard on your next cruise. Once aboard, you can make a hole in your plastic key card and attach the lanyard, allowing you to carry the key around your neck. This is especially useful when your dress or slacks have no pockets. Just be sure to put the hole where it won't interfere with the card's magnetic strip.

Sallie Clinard, Las Vegas, Nev.

NOT SEW I've always traveled with a mini sewing kit in case I needed to sew on a loose button (or replace one). Now when I buy clothes, I just barely touch the end of a tube of Krazy Glue to the front of my buttons. Because they're covered by the glue, the threads don't fray as easily. No more lost buttons!

Calvin Girvin, Texarkana, Tex.

LITTLE BLACK BOOK Before setting off on one of my many backpacking excursions, I head to Kinko's to rebind my guidebook. I replace the cover with a plain black or navy one. It costs about $6 and allows me to blend in much better while traveling. People see my new book as a journal, not a travel guide that labels me a tourist.

Michelle Johnson, Mountain View, Calif.

ANTI-FREEZE Turn off your fridge's ice maker before you leave home. And remember to empty the ice cube bin. The power was out for several days while I was away recently. When I got back, the melted ice had refrozen throughout the freezer compartment. It took forever to clean up.

Mary C. Clements, Durham, N.C.

BOOK MOBILE Before my last long flight, I went to librivox.org and chose a bunch of books, short stories, and poems to download to my iPod—for free. The site has both adult and children's books, and the list is growing. All of the titles are in the public domain, and they're read by volunteers, so there's no question of copyright infringement. Even if you don't own an iPod, you can download them to your computer and burn them onto a CD.

Diane Bowman, Huntington Beach, Calif.

BLACKOUT PATROL < < < < < < < < < <

I live in coastal Florida, where the electricity sometimes goes out during violent storms. Before a trip, I place a few ice cubes in a plastic bag and put the bag in the freezer. If the ice has melted and refrozen by the time I get home, I'll know we've had a power outage and that any food left in the refrigerator may be unsafe to consume.

Brigitte Emick, Daytona Beach, Fla.

MASTER OF YOUR DOMAIN Make a master list of jobs to do around the house before you leave (hold the mail, water the plants, take out the garbage). Keep the list on your computer, print it out, then check off each job as it gets done. You'll be able to go without worrying that you forgot to stop the newspaper.

Glenda McMurray, Georgetown, Ill.

PRESS PAUSE You can suspend more than your newspaper when you're away. On several occasions, DirecTV has agreed to put my account on hold while I was traveling—without penalties, additional fees, reconnection charges, or the like. So, instead of a monthly bill of $65, mine gets prorated.

Ed Clancy, Venice, Calif.

AMASSING POWER Pack a power strip and extension cord for your next cruise. Many cruise-ship cabins have only one outlet, but you'll definitely need more if you want to power up your laptop, iPod, cell phone, electric razor, hairdryer, or any other gadgets you bring on board.

Jay Van Vechten, Boca Raton, Fla.

THE WIPE WAY Tired of catching colds while traveling? Take along a travel-size package of Clorox wipes. Disinfect the tray table and armrests on the airplane, and the telephone and TV remote in your hotel room.

Sherill Hacker, Williamston, Mich.

CHAPTER THREE

ON THE JOURNEY

TRAVELING MADE COMFORTABLE

BUDGET TRAVEL | PAGES 78-95

<BT<<<<<<<<<<<<<<<<<<<<<<<<<<<<
9781594741777<<<<<<<<<<<<<<<<07

INSIDE INFORMATION I work for a major airline and can attest to this tip for redirecting lost luggage. Place a copy of your itinerary—including contact info for where you're staying—inside your checked suitcase. If name and flight tags are missing, we'll still know where your bag needs to go.

Michelle Koenig, Springfield, Mo.

FLEET FEET I switch from street shoes to flannel-lined moccasins at the airport. It saves time at the security checkpoint, and I'm comfortable during the flight. Once I land, I switch back to my street shoes.

John Eymann, League City, Tex.

WORD UP! About a month before leaving on vacation, I start clipping the crossword puzzles from the daily newspaper and pasting them into a blank notebook. The puzzles keep me occupied during my trip. The newspaper's crosswords are so much more interesting than the generic books of them you can purchase at the airport.

Kathie Meyer, Round Rock, Tex.

UNIDENTIFIED FLYING OBJECTS As a flight attendant, I'm always amazed by the stuff that people leave behind. Most of it never gets back to its rightful owner because there's no way of knowing who the owner is. To avoid misplacing your property, put things back into your carry-on after using them—never on the floor or in the seat-back pocket. Label important items like books or games with return address labels so they can be sent back to you if found.

Doug Hummell, Houston, Tex.

SQUIRREL IT AWAY Even if you're not hungry when the flight attendant comes around with the snack service, take it for later. Although peanuts may not look appetizing at 7 a.m., they will look good later if you have nothing better to eat. And it saves you from picking up something at expensive airport shops.

Fran Rifkin, Woodland Hills, Calif.

FRESH FINISH For overnight flights, pack a few Oral B Brush-Ups in your carry-on. Before the plane lands, you can "brush" your teeth, leaving you refreshed and ready for the day!

Janice Pruitt Winfrey, Marietta, Ga.

FROZEN ASSET If you're packing a lunch to eat later in the day, freeze a 16-ounce water bottle and pack it, along with yogurt, cottage cheese, a ham sandwich, or whatever in a lightweight, insulated bag. Your snacks will remain cold, and you can drink the water.

Jackie McGraw, Fort Thomas, Ky.

BEING CENTERED The middle seat isn't always awful. On a recent trip overseas, I called too late to confirm an aisle or window seat. After explaining the plane's AB-CDEFG-HI configuration, the customer service agent urged me to take the very middle seat, E, because D and F have less foot room. (In some rows, there are metal boxes underneath the seats in front of you that house wiring for onboard electronics.) I went along with her advice somewhat skeptically, but I ended up with plenty of room. The people on either side of me weren't so lucky.

Audrey Ting, Secaucus, N.J.

SACRED SOCKS Some international airlines still give passengers a goody bag that includes a toothbrush, an eye mask, and socks for the flight. Keep those socks: They're handy when visiting temples in Thailand, Vietnam, and Cambodia, where you must remove your shoes before entering. I slipped on the socks and my feet stayed both clean and warm!

Nancy Easterbrook, Saratoga, Calif.

QUIET, PLEASE Frequent fliers should consider noise-cancellation headphones. They have a built-in device that "hears" low-frequency sound just before you do and generates a sound wave that cancels it out. Several manufacturers make them, ranging in price from $40 to $300 or so.

Ed Wilhite, Champaign, Ill.

TIRED AND TRUE I always try to work out before heading to the airport. It usually gets me tuckered out enough that I can relax and sleep on the plane. If I don't have time for pretravel exercise, I take a brisk walk through the terminal before boarding or find a quiet spot in an empty gate for a little yoga.

Kimberly Gilbert, Williamstown, Mass.

FLIGHTS AT YOUR FINGERTIPS Download the most up-to-date airline schedules from the individual airline Web sites to your PDA before you leave home. Should you encounter a delay or cancellation at the airport, you'll have all the information needed to find another flight quickly.

Neal Green, Rocky Gorge, Md.

THE RIGHT CALL If your flight is canceled, don't just wait patiently in line to be booked on another flight; call the airline's 800 number. They'll answer your call faster, and you won't be waiting with other stranded passengers from that flight. (Or cover all bases by calling while in line.)

Karen LoPresto-Arbaugh, Kennett Square, Pa.

MAKE DELAYS PAY On a Northwest flight from Wichita to Cleveland, a piece of my luggage was delivered more than a day after I arrived. In the meantime, I had to buy some replacement items. Save your receipts! I turned in the receipts when I checked in for the return flight, and the ticket agent issued me a $50 check. (Northwest allows up to $50 in interim expenses for the first 24 hours, and $25 for each day afterward, with a maximum reimbursement of $150.)

Phil Richard, Hesston, Kans.

VIEW TO A THRILL Book a window seat when you fly to the Caribbean. On a clear day, you can see each island in detail—hills, valleys, and cliffs—as well as the rippling sand underneath the transparent water, in a thousand shades of blue. My recent flight to Barbados was the most incredible in my forty years of travel.

Kathryn Krieger, Orlando, Fla.

SHOWER BY THE HOUR For passengers connecting in Tokyo to other parts of Asia, a chance to freshen up is welcome. The terminals at Narita International Airport offer beds and shower facilities for very reasonable hourly rates. A private room costs about $10 for the first hour and $5 for every hour thereafter. Thirty-minute hot showers run just $5.

Jan Julian, Melbourne, Fla.

CHECK LIST Before you head to the airport, make a list of all the items in your checked luggage that would be prohibited in your carry-on. If an item (such as a knife for a picnic) makes its way into your purse or day pack during your travels, it should be accounted for when repacking and put into the checked piece to avoid hassles at airport security.

Nina Gormley, Bar Harbor, Maine

BOOKMARK IT On international flights, I used to fumble through my belongings—often having to retrieve them from the overhead bin—after a flight attendant appeared with customs and immigration forms. (I don't know of many people who have their passport's number and date of issue memorized.) Now I write all that info on the bookmark of whatever I plan to read on the long flight so I don't have to dig out my passport. I can fill out the card quickly—giving me more time to loan my pen to all the people who never seem to carry one.

Bill Serues, Springtown, Pa.

STEAMY! For long overnight flights, pack a dry washcloth in a Ziploc bag in your carry-on. Before landing, ask the flight attendant for a cup of hot (not boiling) water. Carefully pour the water into the Ziploc bag and then wipe your face and hands with the steaming cloth. It's like a portable sauna!

Henrietta Scarlett Ober, Charlotte, Vt.

PILLOW TALK Therm-a-Rest's Compressible Pillow is perfect for the plane. It comes in three sizes, packs smaller and expands bigger than any other pillow, and is machine washable. Whenever I pull mine out of my carry-on, I get jealous stares: People always ask where they can get one. REI sells the pillows for $18 to $25, depending on the size (rei.com).

Sheila Lauber, Anderson Island, Wash.

CHECK IN AT CHECK-OUT Before you head to the airport, stop by the front desk of your hotel or cruise ship and ask if they'll print your boarding pass for you. It'll save Internet browsing fees and time at check-in. It's worked for me at several Marriott hotels and on a Celebrity cruise.

Rose Jakubaszek, Jersey City, N.J.

PROOF OF PURCHASE Before you leave the United States, photocopy receipts for any expensive items you're taking with you. This way, you won't have to argue with customs on the way home about declaring items you didn't buy abroad. (I'm a photographer, and I always bring expensive cameras on vacations.)

Derrick Du, Livermore, Calif.

VIS-À-VIS VISAS If you're headed to a country that requires a visa, ask the consulate of that country, in the United States, whether visas are also issued at the airport there on arrival. In many cases (like Turkey and Egypt), they are. Obtaining the visa on arrival is a much simpler procedure and a real money-saver: You do not have to have photographs taken (they figure your passport already has a photo), you do not pay a hefty fee to the U.S.-situated consulate of the country, you avoid the expense and risk of mailing your passport to that consulate in advance of departure, and you avoid the expense of using a visa-acquiring company in the United States. But be sure the consulate is correct that the visa can easily be obtained on arrival.

Carmencita Soriano, San Diego, Calif.

HAVING A BALL A beach ball can replace many expensive in-flight gadgets. Depending on how much you inflate it, the ball can function as a very comfortable footrest, a back support, or a lap pillow to support your book.

Dorothy Vincent, New York, N.Y.

BLANK CHECK Be certain to have enough blank pages in your passport. Someone I know had a terrible time getting permission to board a flight from Zambia to South Africa because she didn't have the two blank passport pages required to enter South Africa. Thank goodness my husband had read about the requirement. Before the trip, we sent our passports to the center in Charleston and had extra pages added at no charge.

Patricia Beagle, Williamsville, N.Y.

EXPIRATION SITUATION If you're traveling overseas, be sure to check the fine print concerning passports (go online or call the country's embassy). I had three months before my passport expired and found out at the last minute that I needed six months' leeway to enter Tahiti. Luckily, I was able to get a new passport just in time for my vacation.

Jean Schwinn, Sauk Rapids, Minn.

SINGLED OUT If you're divorced and plan to travel out of the country with your children, check the legal requirements in advance. When I tried to take my kids to Cancún, I learned too late that Mexico requires a notarized letter of consent signed by both parents for minors traveling alone or with one parent or guardian. If the parents are divorced, a copy of the parental custody agreement is allowed instead. The airlines enforce this rule before you get on the plane.

Marge Stratton, Big Flats, N.Y.

JUST ADD MILK Finding healthy breakfast alternatives at an airport can prove difficult. I always travel with an insulated travel mug. Before leaving home I fill it with a high-protein cereal and then request low-fat milk on the flight.

Randy Hartselle, Lincoln, Calif.

WALK AND ROLL Treat yourself to a golf-ball foot massage. During a long flight, or afterward in your hotel room, take off your shoes, put a golf ball on the floor, and roll it under your foot. It's a great stress reliever. Practice a bit before you try it on a plane, so that your ball doesn't go rolling down the cabin, tripping up unsuspecting passengers.

Dawn Yadlosky, Centerville, Ohio

ROUTE FOR THE HOME TEAM Every summer, we drive out West from Pennsylvania with our two kids. To avoid that infamous road trip question ("Are we there yet?"), I give each child a map with our route highlighted on it. Along the way, they can match up the town names with road signs we pass, and that way, they always know exactly where we are and how much farther we have to go until we'll get there.

Machell McCoy, Carlisle, Pa.

DISTRACTING ACT When traveling with your kids, give each child his or her own small carry-on bag. Fill it with new, surprise treats to occupy the downtime—layovers, long flights, time in hotels—as well as a few familiar items from home. Include a notebook and encourage your child to keep a travel diary.

Joan White, Dallas, Tex.

SCHOOL FOR SCAMPERING If you're on a road trip with young children and you're looking for a place to let them blow off some steam, check out the playgrounds at local elementary schools. They almost always have equipment that your children will love to explore. It will also give everyone in the family a welcome chance to stretch their legs.

Heather Fitzgerald, Little Compton, R.I.

TOYING AROUND Put toys within kids' reach on road trips. Hang a shoe organizer on the back of the passenger seat so children can keep stuffed animals, books, and games organized in the pockets. Having everything close at hand may help prevent meltdowns along the way.

Jennifer Casasanto, Newton, Mass.

ZIP RIGHT THROUGH Just before I go through airport security, to save time and to avoid leaving something important behind, I collect all loose items—change, money clip, belt buckle, pens—in a large Ziploc bag. I send the bag through the X-ray machine with the rest of my luggage. After picking it up at the other end, I put the things back in place and either toss the bag or keep it for the return trip.

Rodrigo Fernandez, Ewing, N.J.

CHAPTER FOUR

<BT<<<<<<<<<<<<<<<<<<<<<<<<<<<<
9781594741777<<<<<<<<<<<<<<<<07

ALL ACCOUNTED FOR If you're planning to use an ATM abroad, make sure the money you need is in your checking account, because some foreign ATMs don't allow access to savings accounts. And remember to carry your bank's local phone number with you; 800 numbers generally don't work overseas.

Donna Johnson, Bridgeport, Conn.

FANTASTIC FOUR Some people think that traveler's checks aren't necessary anymore, but they really can be useful in a variety of situations. My ATM card wouldn't work on Easter Island, where most restaurants did not accept credit cards and wanted to be paid in pesos. Luckily, our hotel cashed my traveler's checks and gave me the pesos I needed. On Dominica, my purse was stolen. But because I had traveler's checks stashed away in my luggage, the vacation wasn't ruined. I always travel with what I call the "trusty four": American dollars (lots of ones and fives divided up and hidden in several locations), traveler's checks, an ATM card, and a credit card.

Jeanette Cantwell, Poughkeepsie, N.Y.

EXTRA CREDIT When my husband and I travel, we take at least three different credit cards. I carry one he doesn't have, he carries one I don't have, and we both bring our primary card. If one of us has our wallet stolen, we can cancel two cards and still have one to use. We each have different ATM cards, too—useful if a machine doesn't honor one of the cards, or if we need more cash than our daily limit allows.

Joyce Morden, Port Angeles, Wash.

A TAXING GOODBYE Before exchanging foreign currency at the airport, find out if there's a departure tax. At the Bangkok airport, we were very upset—as were travelers around us—to find we had to pay a fee before continuing to our gate. Unfortunately, by that point everyone had cashed in their baht, so the options were a conveniently located ATM, a credit card, or an exchange booth with notably poor rates. When we described this incident to friends, they told us of a similar experience when trying to leave the Dominican Republic.

Parisa Montazeri, Bridgewater, Va.

VALID DATES Note the expiration dates of any debit or credit cards you plan on using while you're away. In Budapest, I tried to withdraw cash with my ATM card, only to find that it had expired just days before.

Matt Vance, Austin, Tex.

SAFETY PIN Know your PINs! My husband and I left home with very little cash on us, and instead of stopping to get money at the airport, my husband—ever the procrastinator—decided to wait until we got to Cancún to use his ATM card. Guess what? It didn't work in any of the machines. And although he had several credit cards for cash advances, he didn't know the PINs off the top of his head. We charged everything we could during our stay, but most of the markets don't take credit cards. Needless to say, I didn't come home with a lot of souvenirs.

CaSandra Knight, Crestview, Fla.

DAILY BREAD When on vacation, I split my cash into envelopes, one per day, so I can keep track of how much I'm spending. If I need to dig into the next day's cash, I'll know that I've overdone it, and if I want to stay on budget, I'll have to cut back the next day. Any money left at the end of the day goes into a separate envelope. I've actually come home with money this way!

Wendy L. Phiel, Exton, Pa.

PURSES APLENTY If I plan to travel to several countries that use different currencies, I pack a few cloth change purses: U.S. dollars go into one, British pounds in another, euros in a third, etc. When I'm sightseeing, I carry only the money I need; the purses that I'm not using are locked away in the hotel safe. I avoid fumbling around in shops and mixing up coins that look alike. Plus, I always know exactly how much cash I have.

Peg Welch, York, Pa.

SHARE YOUR SCHEDULE <<<<<<<<

We always e-mail our itinerary—including flights, hotels, and confirmation numbers—to ourselves and to family members. If our luggage is lost or our wallets are stolen, all of this essential information is just an Internet café and a few quick clicks away.

Courtney Fuller, Atlanta, Ga.

LAUNDERED MONEY We've traveled to both Mexico and China in the last year and had the same experience in both countries: When we tried to exchange dollars to local currency, the banks wouldn't take bills with graffiti on them—telephone numbers, names, doodles, anything. Nor would they accept any bills that were torn or damaged. (We noticed a group from France having the same problem with their euros.) So before you leave home, make sure that any money you plan on exchanging is absolutely crisp and clean—or better yet, ask your bank specifically for brand-new bills.

John Rybczyk, The Villages, Fla.

THE BEST POLICY Quotetravelinsurance.com gives you comparable details on more than one hundred travel-insurance plans, enabling you to make the best buy. It relies on ratings from insurance industry overseers such as A.M. Best and state insurance commissioners before allowing an insurance company into its extensive lineup.

Marc Oppy, Portland, Ore.

DOORSTOP PROP If you're a woman traveling alone, or your accommodations don't inspire confidence, simply wedge a small rubber doorstop at the base of the door when you're inside the room. It'll be virtually impossible to open the door from the outside.

Kimberly Milne-Fowler, Denmark, Australia

ID YOUR PC We were told by an airport security official to tape a business card onto the cover of our laptop. Turns out he has an average of six laptop computers left behind each day! There are so many more procedures now—removing shoes, removing coats—that people forget when they send their laptop through in a separate bin. The official added that it's very difficult to return them because most laptops have passwords that keep the owners' personal information hidden.

Liz Nealon, New York, N.Y.

TIMING IS MONEY < < < < < < < < < <

If you arrive in a foreign city after banking hours (and you can't use an ATM), convert only the money you'll need for the night. Some exchange booths offer a less favorable rate after banks close and then switch back to competitive rates when banks reopen.

Jim Citron, West Lebanon, N.H.

POCKET PROTECTOR A simple but effective antipickpocketing measure is to fasten a safety pin across the opening of the pants pocket on the inside. Leave enough room to pull your wallet out with some effort, but not enough for a quick hand to lift it in a second or two.

Rusty Cartmill, Alpharetta, Ga.

LESS IS MORE Rather than risk losing your department-store credit cards and club-membership cards, you should really leave them behind when you go somewhere you won't need them. Your purse or wallet will be lighter and your worries fewer.

George Bracken, Ilion, N.Y.

KNOW WHERE TO GO If you're traveling with someone, discuss a central meeting place in case you get separated. My husband and I were in Paris waiting to board the Métro. He was able to board the train, but I was left behind on the platform. Having a plan saved both time and needless anxiety.

Marian Moss, Stone Mountain, Ga.

SLIP-UP I bought several items while in London and noticed when I returned home that my credit card number was printed in full on each sales slip. (In the United States, usually only the last four digits of the number are visible.) Travelers should be careful when using their credit cards overseas—don't leave the sales slips lying around.

Jackie MacNeil, Santa Maria, Calif.

LUGGAGE LOCKDOWN Pack a couple of mountaineering carabiners. Clip one through the handle or strap of your bag and secure it to something solid wherever you may be (to a bench in the park or in a train station, to the railing of an overhead compartment on a bus, etc.). The carabiner adds a bit of security, especially if you're snoozing.

R. Bryan Simon, Roanoke, Va.

WARNING BELLS In order to keep track of my bags, I use a small metal bell—the kind dancers from India wear on their ankles. I thread it with fishing line and tie it to my carry-on. If anyone touches my bag after I set it down, the bell chimes. It's not a very obtrusive sound, but it's distinctive enough for me to notice if a thief is trying to get into my things. The same bell can be hung on the doorknob inside your hotel room.

Jim Hall, Buford, Ga.

RING ENGAGEMENT A padlocked zipper tells thieves there's something in your bag worth stealing, but a key ring is much less obvious. Just use it to latch together the zippers. Best of all, you'll never have to worry about forgetting your combination.

France Freeman, Seattle, Wash.

STEAL TRAP Our bags have been stolen twice from inside locked rental cars. Now we travel with a bicycle cable and lock. If we absolutely have to leave our suitcases in the car, I hook them together by the handles and attach the whole thing to the frame of a seat or a secure item in the trunk. Even if thieves manage to get into our car, the cable will make it very difficult for them to make off with the luggage.

Karen McCarty, McCall, Idaho

STRINGS ATTACHED I'm a gadget freak, and I don't like to travel without things like my digital camera and iPod. On one trip, though, I put my camera down in a crowded restaurant and then forgot to put it back in my bag. By the time I remembered it, the camera was long gone. Now, I attach those kinds of items to my daypack with a lanyard. They're still easy to pull out and use, and they never get left behind.

France Freeman, Seattle, Wash.

TRAY CHIC We all know to avoid drinking tap water in certain countries, but remember to forgo ice cubes, too. I've started bringing along two ice trays, which I fill with bottled water and freeze in my hotel room's minifridge.

Christa Babel, Lakewood, Colo.

SEAL OF APPROVAL < < < < < < < < < <

When buying bottled water, look at the bottle cap to see if the seal is still intact. While visiting the Acropolis on a very hot day this summer, I caught a young boy refilling empty water bottles from a tap and recapping them. He was then selling the bottles to thirsty tourists.

Alice Atkinson, Houston, Tex.

ALLERGIC ACTION Traveling to non-English-speaking countries can be daunting for people with food allergies. Find someone fluent in the local language to write out what you are allergic to, the seriousness of the allergy (we had a friend include the phrase "this could kill me"), and what to do if you fall ill.

M. Thompson and K. A. Fares Bannon, London, Ont.

POST FACTO Most British post offices will allow you to change foreign currency without any commission charges. This is particularly useful for changing euros and U.S. dollars to pounds sterling and back again. To locate a branch near where you're staying, log on to postoffice.co.uk.

Angela Skelcher, London, UK

PILL POP-IN Don't be afraid to go to a foreign pharmacy. I forgot to pack my prescription medication on a recent trip to France. When my problem acted up, I went to a local pharmacy. (Look for the green cross.) The pharmacist provided my medication without a prescription and at a fraction of what it would have cost in the United States. In fact, one could benefit by stocking up abroad on medications that would normally be acquired at home at a much higher price.

Mainard Tom, Sunnyvale, Calif.

1-800-WONT-WRK Before traveling overseas, look at your health insurance card. If it only shows an 800 or 888 number for precertification of hospital admissions, call that number and obtain the local number with an area code. Many 800 numbers can't be dialed from foreign countries. I learned this the hard way during an emergency hospital admission in Switzerland. The delay in reaching my carrier could have been avoided.

Chris Carveth, Orange, Conn.

GIVING AID The day before we left Zanzibar, Tanzania, we donated our very well-equipped first-aid kit to a nonprofit organization that cares for the elderly. The people there were extremely grateful to receive our unused antibiotics, nonprescription pain remedies, assorted bandages, antiseptic sprays, and ointments. And it really felt great to give something back to the community before heading home.

Janet Barton, Sausalito, Calif.

RUBBED THE WRONG WAY? If you start to feel a painful blister coming on, put some lip balm or Vaseline on the hot spot—it'll help stop the rubbing.

Donna Benesch, Cincinnati, Ohio

ALL IN THE WRIST Place a coin over the veins on the inside of your wrist (about two finger widths from the base of your palm) and secure it in place with a rubber band or ponytail holder. The gentle pressure of the coin will stimulate nerves that control nausea, just like the motion-sickness bands that are sold at drugstores.

Connie Crusha, El Cajon, Calif.

GREAT WIPE HOPE I don't go anywhere without individual packets of antibacterial wipes. I slip some in my carry-on, day-pack, and shirt pocket. They're very convenient when you can't find any running water with which to wash your hands. And because they're antibacterial, they're also great for cleaning cuts, and the alcohol from the wipes helps stop the itching when you rub them on insect bites.

Lawrence Brenner, Schertz, Tex.

GENERIC ADVICE I agree that the antiseasickness medication for cruises, Bonine, is excellent and effective; but there is a budget way to buy it. The primary ingredient in Bonine is meclizine (25 mg). While a package of eight Bonine tablets costs just over $4 at a drugstore, you can buy a bottle of 100 generic meclizine (25 mg) for about the same price. This is an over-the-counter (no prescription needed) item, but you usually have to ask for it at the pharmacy counter.

Lila Held, Garden Grove, Calif.

PHOTO PROTECTED Ever since my children were small, I've carried recent, wallet-size pictures of them when we all go on vacation, in case we get separated. Now that they are teenagers and traveling with friends' families, too, I send pictures for the other family to bring along with them. I also write my telephone numbers on the back of the pictures so they know where to reach me in an emergency.

Ruth Ann Newsum, Hutchinson, Kans.

STAT SHEET Create an ID page for each of your children before you leave on a trip. In addition to vacation contact information (hotel name and phone number), include the child's name, a current photo, home address, phone, date of birth, Social Security number, passport number, hair color, eye color, height, any identifying marks, blood type, allergies, medications, doctor and insurance phone numbers and ID numbers, immunization schedule, and fingerprints (these don't change, so investing the time to have a set made is worth it). If the unspeakable happens, the ability to hand over instant, concise information to authorities may prove invaluable. Update it before every trip.

Robin Flannery, Riverhead, N.Y.

JUST SAY "BLOW" Give your children a coach's whistle in case they get lost; put it on a ribbon so they can wear it around their neck. The piercing sound may be annoying, but you'll definitely find them quicker!

Chandra Huang, Honolulu, Hawaii

KIDS' KIT When traveling with my kids, I bring a Ziploc bag that includes four things: Benadryl, children's ibuprofen, one of those little medicine cups, and a thermometer. This all-purpose kit will help with minor ailments, or treat a more serious flu until you can get to a doctor. Best of all, it saves Dad from driving around at 2 a.m. looking for an all-night pharmacy.

Heather Crow, Rio Rancho, N.M.

ROLL WITH IT Having spent a number of years working for Norwegian Cruise Line, I learned that a dinner roll helps to settle the stomach when seas become rough. The less liquid sloshing around unimpeded, the better. And if you forget your motion-sickness pills or wristbands, fear not, as the purser always has medicine available for seasick passengers.

Jim Polanzke, York, Pa.

COLD CALL Paramedics now look for emergency contact information in victims' mobile phones. Store the word "ICE" (In Case of Emergency) in your address book, along with the name and number of the person you'd like emergency personnel to call on your behalf. (For more than one entry, use ICE1, ICE2, etc.) Tell your friends or family members that you've chosen them as your contacts and make sure they're aware of any medical conditions or allergies that could affect your treatment.

Cindy Nguyen, Chicago, Ill.

TUB TROUBLE Grab-rails and nonskid surfaces aren't common in European bathtubs and showers. I pack a few decorative rubber pads that have nonadhesive suction cups, so I can use them when needed to prevent a slip or fall, and then I take them with me to the next hotel.

Fran Plewak, Warren, Vt.

HELLO KITTY My friends and I contribute to a kitty and use that money to pay for group expenses such as taxis and meals. It saves us from having to figure out each person's share at every stop. At the end of the trip, we split what remains.

Carol Moran, Chesterfield, Mo.

WATERPROOF BARRIER Whenever I'm in a country where drinking or brushing my teeth with the tap water is a risk, I cover the faucet handles in my hotel bathroom with a towel. As a result, I never accidentally turn on the faucet when I'm half asleep.

Denise Crocker, Millbrae, Calif.

CHAPTER FIVE

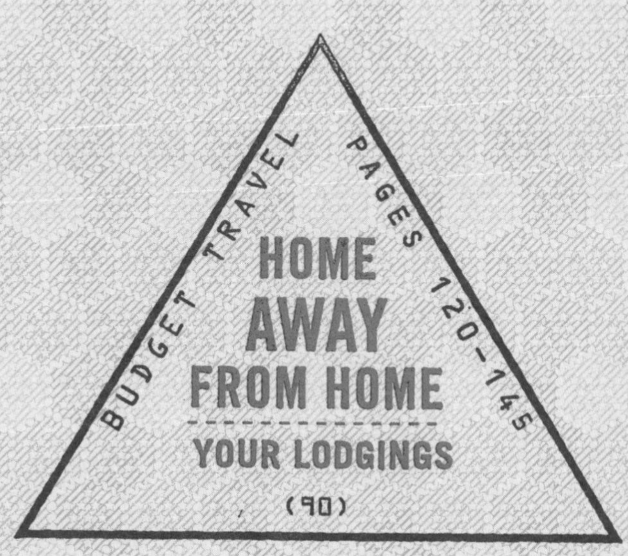

<BT<<<<<<<<<<<<<<<<<<<<<<<<<<<<<<<
9781594741777<<<<<<<<<<<<<<<<<<<07

SHOWER DROUGHT When I was in China, the water shut off while I was taking a shower. It was only then I realized that the empty bucket in the bathtub was there for a reason: I should have filled it with water to prepare for just such an event.

Ned Clem, Carefree, Ariz.

IN-DEPTH KNOWLEDGE Scuba-diving vacations can get expensive. As I start planning a trip, I call one of the local PADI dive shops and ask the employees about accommodations nearby. They give me hotel connections I couldn't find on my own, and I often save enough to pay for my dives.

Lyle Bennett, Murfreesboro, Tenn.

SHUTTLED SHUTTLE Remember to check the hours of operation for your hotel's airport shuttle. In Rome, we were surprised to learn that our hotel—which touted its shuttle—only offered the service a few hours a day.

Gail Moriarty, Waterbury, Conn.

A BLANK SHEET When I'm packing to leave a hotel room, I turn the bedding down to the foot of the bed so that the white sheets are facing up. This way, items placed on the bed are clearly visible. I once left a camera behind because I couldn't see it against a very dark bedspread.

Fran Schaak, Grand Rapids, Mich.

ONLINE FIND Before you book a room over the phone, peruse the hotel's site for its "Web only" rate. It's often cheaper than the best quote you'll get by calling. Recently, over the phone, I was quoted a daily rate of $129. I booked the same room online for $89.

Ying Wang, Ellicott City, Md.

MEMBERS ONLY Sign up for guest programs at every hotel chain that offers one, even if you haven't stayed at that hotel before or think you may not travel enough to reap benefits from multiple stays. Some programs send coupons for discounted rooms or complimentary room upgrades just for being a member. After signing up for the Omni Hotels Select Guest program, I received a coupon that I was able to redeem for a room in Chicago for $80 per night.

Allison Meyer, Chicago, Ill.

RESORT TO IT Even if you're staying at a standard resort hotel, take advantage of the day passes sold by many all-inclusive resorts (i.e., the right to use their facilities—such as swimming pools and beach chairs—and enjoy their meals for a day). The passes are primarily designed for cruise passengers on day trips but can be obtained by anyone for very little money. For persons staying in a less-expensive, no-frills hotel, it can give you the experience of a larger, more extensive resort for a day or two.

Mandy Vieregg, Waco, Tex.

UNCONVENTIONAL WISDOM When you go to a convention or trade show, don't assume that the official prices at recommended hotels are the best you can do. Go to the hotel Web site. I recently got an AARP rate at a major hotel that was 30 percent below the special price offered through the trade-show sponsors. AAA discounts often work, too.

Duane Dahl, Santa Fe, N.M.

CASHING IN Try getting a discount on your hotel room by offering to pay in cash. A hotel reservationist suggested this approach when I phoned to reserve at a hotel in London. I asked if the hotel could grant a discount based on my AARP or AAA membership, as many hotels do in the United States. Her response was that the only discount she was able to offer was 10 percent if I paid in cash.

Joan Nikelsky, Upper Darby, Pa.

LOTS OF PARKING You can enjoy free airport-area parking by staying the night before departure at an airport hotel or motel that offers park-and-fly rates. The cost of that overnight (which usually entitles you to two weeks of parking) is much less than what you'd otherwise pay at an airport parking lot.

Mike Zaloudek, Los Angeles, Calif.

DOUBLE HAPPINESS Don't assume a single room costs less than a double one. I booked a hotel in Spain online and noticed that rates were the same whether I booked a single or a double, but the single was much smaller and its bathroom had only a small shower stall and no tub.

Don Carne, Lansing, Mich.

TAKE YOURSELF TO THE CLEANERS Instead of dropping my laundry off at the front desk, I take a walk around the block and look for the nearest dry cleaner—probably the same one the hotel would've taken it to. By cutting out the middleman, I pay a quarter of what they charge at the hotel!

Amy Parks, Raleigh, N.C.

NOT SO SWIMMINGLY < < < < < < < < < <

My family and I made reservations for a beach condo on Maui. Upon arrival, we were shocked to see a sign at the beach that read No Swimming. Make certain you specify a swimming beach when booking a vacation rental.

Ruth Herlean, Richmond, Va.

DRY IDEA Cold-weather traveling means turning up the thermostat in your hotel room, and along with the artificially warmed air come dry skin and static electricity. Instead of turning on the heat, fill the bathtub with very hot water and leave the bathroom door open. In about an hour, your entire room will be warm and humidified.

Susan Mutty, Holt, Mich.

WHAT'S MY LINER? I was heading to the hotel ice machine when I noticed that our ice bucket was looking very tired and missing its disposable plastic liner. My solution: the shower cap that we never use anyway. In fact, it actually worked better than the liner bag because the elastic band held it in place around the top of the bucket.

Susan Swickard, Estes Park, Colo.

MAT MUFFLER I've found that by wedging a bath mat under my hotel-room door, I can reduce any light or noise coming from the hallway—ensuring that I'll sleep better.

Louisa Elder, Northbrook, Ill.

BEAT THE CLOCK Before you go to sleep, check to see if a previous hotel guest left the alarm clock on. I've been awakened before 7 a.m. twice in the last couple of months by alarms I did not set. (Make sure the clock shows the right time, too!)

Rachele Hemphill, Napa, Calif.

CONDO ATTITUDE Booking condos last minute can yield incredible bargains, and there's a way to maximize savings while minimizing the risk that you won't find a room at all. ("Last minute" generally means a month or less before your stay; seven-day deals usually start on a Saturday.) Buy your plane ticket and book a refundable hotel room you can use in case you can't find that bargain condo. Then, a month or so before your trip, start looking at last-minute sites—lastminutetravel.com, site59.com, etc. If you find a deal, simply get a refund on the hotel room and pay the cancellation fee, if there happens to be one. Using this technique, I found a great beachfront, one-bedroom condo on Maui—and I saved about $300.

Joan Chyun, Irvine, Calif.

BRIGHT IDEA I always bring a small flashlight to hotels in case there's a blackout. The building may not be equipped with emergency lighting, and, if necessary, my flashlight will help me quickly locate the nearest exit.

Louis Meshonek, Cedarhurst, N.Y.

SKIRTING THE ISSUE Flight attendants often work vampire hours and have to sleep during the day. How do we keep the sunlight from leaking into our hotel rooms? We clip a skirt hanger (or two) to the middle of the drapes to seal them together.

Elisabeth Joyce, San Clemente, Calif.

UPGRADE YOURSELF If you're stranded overnight at an airport and receive a "distress rate" voucher, call the hotel of your choice before blindly following the airline's suggestion. You may find that for that discounted rate (or a few bucks more) you can stay in a hotel with a lot more amenities than the one the airline would put you in. After a long, mishap-filled trip, anyone can appreciate a really good mattress, a top-notch restaurant, and an indoor swimming pool.

Carlos Martinez, Houston, Tex.

SKEETER SHOOING There's nothing worse than trying to fall asleep under a mosquito net and then realizing that the bugs are finding a way inside. So next time you're heading someplace tropical—where you know you'll be sleeping under mosquito netting—remember to toss a roll of Scotch tape into your suitcase. It's perfect for quick repairs.

Christopher Swain, East Point, Ga.

NORDIC NIGHTS If you are planning a trip to northern Europe, check out bedandbreakfast.dk. In Denmark, for instance, you can choose from nearly four hundred properties located all over the country. Rooms generally run from $55 to $80 per night for two people (Copenhagen can cost slightly more), and usually include a full European breakfast of coffee, juice, breads, cheese, and hard-boiled eggs.

Nancy J. Mayland, Auburn, N.H.

BIG IN JAPAN When you travel through Japan, stay at members of the Toyoko Inn chain (toyoko-inn.com/eng). Though billed as limited-amenity business hotels, they provide large, clean, and functional rooms (most with Continental or Japanese-style breakfast and free Internet) for around $60.

Brian Yokoyama, Pomona, Calif.

AT HOME IN LONDON With londonbb.com, you can find single rooms in Londoners' homes at affordable prices (starting at about $45). I stayed in a tiny bedroom in a lovely house in the elegant Hampstead neighborhood. My bedroom was on its own little landing of the house and was supremely quiet and private. It also had a TV and a view of the garden.

Bonnie A. Marston, Lynnwood, Wash.

FOREIGN THINKING Traveling to Great Britain, you can save a considerable amount on your lodgings by accessing the UK Web sites of hotel chains. For example, travelodge.co.uk has a section for offers and competitions with rates starting at $29 per room (not per person).

Amy B. Cochran, Fort Edward, N.Y.

VILLA VALUES To find a reasonably priced villa or apartment to rent, try going directly to the owner through a site such as abritel.fr. (Click on the British flag for English.) I arranged to spend two weeks in an apartment in Brittany and one week in an apartment in the Loire Valley, all for a total of $800.

Suzanne Maurice-Roberts, Staunton, Va.

SPINE-CHILLING If you can't sleep due to the heat in your non-air-conditioned hotel room, take a cold bottle of water and place it on your pillow, in the crook of your neck. It will cool your whole body down.

Tony van Hasselt, East Boothbay, Maine

A PRESSING MATTER When I'm on the road, I often have to use the hotel iron before heading out to business meetings. But getting water into the iron can be a hassle—most irons won't fit under the sink faucet, and using a glass to pour water into the tiny hole is nearly impossible without spilling everywhere. There's an easy solution: Use the carafe from the coffee maker. Just be sure the carafe is clean, or you could end up with coffee stains on your clothes.

Paul Schnebelen, Oxnard, Calif.

ROOM FOR NEGOTIATION <<<<<<<

When I called to book a hotel room in Budapest, I was offered a rate of $75 per night. After I told the concierge that I was looking for a room in the $35 range, he agreed to the lower price without much fuss. It sometimes pays to barter.

Julie Jensen, Madison, Wis.

TIP AT THE TOP If you plan to leave a gratuity for hotel staff, follow our friend Phil's good advice: Give it at the beginning of your vacation, not at the end. He introduces himself to the housekeepers early in the trip and hands them a nice tip. Guess who always has plenty of coffee and fresh towels?

Lou Stover, Cardiff, Calif.

MAKE NICE TO THE MAID On the final day of a recent Caribbean vacation, I tried to arrange for a late checkout, but was told it wasn't possible. The hotel offered me the use of a day-room; it would have been perfect, but it was being used by other guests, and there was a very long wait for the shower. I went back upstairs and saw that someone was just about to clean my room. I told the housekeeper that I understood she had to do her job, but I wondered if I could I take a quick shower first. She offered to clean next door while I took my shower. I tipped her $10 and then left for the airport.

Michele Chico, Staten Island, N.Y.

FILL 'ER UP! Before you buy expensive bottled water from your hotel room minibar, head to the fitness center. You'll be able to fill up an empty bottle at the gym's water cooler or fountain for free, and you don't need to break a sweat.

Amanda Geraci, Atlanta, Ga.

READY, SET, GLOW Finding the bathroom in the middle of the night in a strange hotel room or cruise-ship cabin can be a challenge. Leaving the bathroom light on seems wasteful and makes the room too bright for sleeping. My husband and I used to travel with a night-light, but we couldn't always find a convenient place to plug it in. We've recently discovered a better solution: plastic light sticks. They come in several glow-in-the-dark colors and are activated by bending the tube into a circle and connecting the ends. Each evening, we hook one of the loops over the bathroom-door handle, where it provides a gentle glow through the night.

Carol Attar, Grosse Pointe Woods, Mich.

BEDSIDE MANNER If you're traveling solo and your room has a double bed, sleep on the side farthest from the phone. It's slept on less frequently and is therefore more comfortable.

Ruth Schnur, Princeton, N.J.

THE LITTLE BOY'S ROOM When my husband and I would stay in a hotel with our two-year-old, a full night's sleep was out of the question. The minute our son opened his eyes (at 2, 3, or 4 a.m.), he woke us, thinking it was time to play. We now pack a pop-up tent and set it up in a corner of the hotel room with books, a blanket, and a few small stuffed animals. The tent folds down to a 14-inch circle and weighs about a pound. It works great! My son has his own "room" to sleep in when we vacation, and we all get to sleep through the night!

Geri Kronyak, Boonton, N.J.

DRAWER YOUR OWN CONCLUSION Need a place for a laptop in your hotel room? Take the largest drawer from the bureau and put it upside down on the bed with the drawer front away from you. This creates a perfect-height desk for while you're sitting comfortably on the bed (you can even lean back on pillows), plus there's side space for papers, and the top leans toward you for easy typing or writing.

Linda Diebold Johnson, Larose, La.

GYM DANDY If you take an overnight flight to Europe and early check-in at your hotel isn't an option, ask the concierge if you can store your luggage until later in the day and use the hotel gym's shower. You'll be refreshed and ready for sightseeing. Pack toiletries and a change of clothes in your carry-on.

Brian Huseman, Washington, D.C.

RUBBER DUCKY NOT INCLUDED It can be difficult for parents to find a place to bathe their infant while on vacation. Showers obviously won't work, and the miniscule sinks generally found in hotel bathrooms aren't appropriate either. On our last cruise, we eliminated the whole problem by packing a small, inexpensive inflatable bathtub. (Ours cost only $7.99.) When we arrived, we blew it up and placed it in the bottom of the shower for an instant, safe baby bath.

Maria Diekema-Zuidema, Lewisville, N.C.

PEDI-CURE Most hotels provide cloth shoe mitts but not polish. In a pinch, a dollop of skin cream on a shoe mitt (or even a tissue) can make scuff marks vanish and leave shoes as shiny as if they'd been cleaned by a pro.

John Nechman, Humble, Tex.

AUTO-DIAL I have the words "hotel" and "taxi" on my cellphone speed dial. On a trip, I change the numbers, but leave the preprogrammed titles the same—instant access and no more little slips of paper everywhere.

Isabel Burk, New City, N.Y.

FUZZ BUSTER I unpacked a pair of black slacks recently to find them covered with white fuzz. I didn't have a lint brush handy, so I used the luggage sticker from my bag—the gummy side took the lint right off.

Joyce Barbatti, Cedar Falls, Iowa

MORE WIRE HANGERS! The couple of hangers provided on cruise ships aren't enough for weeklong trips. So I save wire hangers from the dry cleaner and slip a few into our suitcases while packing. I then leave them behind for the next passenger.

Wendy Maloney, Vienna, Va.

SHOE-IN A shoe organizer hung over the bathroom door is my solution for hotel-room clutter. The compartments are perfect for stashing everything from room keys and travel documents to toiletries and, of course, shoes. The extra storage space came in especially handy on a recent cruise, when we needed all the room we could get in our tiny cabin.

Jane Tague, Westerville, Ohio

ON THE RIGHT FOOT Save the flip-flops you're given at the nail salon after a pedicure. They make great shower shoes. They're lightweight and dry quickly, and you can throw them away at the end of your trip.

Carmen Shirkey, Fairfax, Va.

YOU'LL BE HOOKED I find that hotel bathrooms rarely have enough hangers and hooks for clothes and wet towels, so I always bring a few snap-lock suction hooks. (They function better than regular suction hooks because they're more secure and are therefore able to hold heavier items.) It's always nice to have a place to hang a bathrobe.

Laura Tillman, Northville, Mich.

GET STUCK The magnets you use on a refrigerator will also stick well to most hotel- and motel-room doors, turning them into makeshift bulletin boards. Post theater tickets, itineraries, reminder notes, and any other useful information, then grab what you need before you leave the room for the day.

Karen Hartz, Millersville, Md.

MUST NOT On my first trip to Cancún, I noticed that my hotel room had a damp, musty odor. The next time I went, I brought two plug-in air fresheners: one for the bedroom and one for the bathroom. This helped tremendously. It was a pleasure to walk in and have a fresh-smelling room. Just make sure you have an adapter, if you need one.

Anita Rivera, Deltona, Fla.

CHAPTER SIX

<BT<<<<<<<<<<<<<<<<<<<<<<<<<<<<
9781594741777<<<<<<<<<<<<<<<<07

PICK OF THE LOT Online check-in isn't just for airlines. After reserving an Alamo car over the Internet, I was offered online check-in just by entering my credit card number and driver's license information for approval. At the airport, following Alamo's instructions, I informed the shuttle-bus driver that I had checked in online and reserved an economy car. I was dropped off in the lot and told to pick whichever car I wanted. I drove it to the exit, where my credit card and driver's license were verified on the computer, and I was done.

Brad Cook, Colorado Springs, Colo.

AAA-OK I've saved lots of money using AAA. In addition to providing excellent roadside services (help with stalled cars, lost keys, etc.), most AAA chapters offer discounted tickets to Disney World and a preferred parking pass that enables you to grab specially designated spots near the entrances. It's a dollar saver, and you don't have to walk far or take the trolley in the parks!

Judy Small, Cicero, Ind.

NO LUGGAGE-LUGGING If you've accumulated more souvenirs on your trip than you can carry, drive your rental car up to curbside check-in, then return the vehicle and come back on the shuttle bus with only your carry-on. This only works if there's no check-in line, but can save dragging your luggage onto the shuttle bus, across parking lots, etc.

Robyn Volkening, Brighton, Colo.

DAMAGE CONTROL When renting a car, photograph any damage the car may have before leaving the rental agency; a digital camera records the date and time of each picture. On a recent trip to Argentina, I rented a car with extensive paint damage. When I returned the car, the agency attempted to blame me for the scratches. I showed them my photographs, and they rescinded their accusations.

Richard L. Garcia Jr., San Antonio, Tex.

FLAG WAVING I always have problems locating my rental car in a large parking lot. Now I bring along a brightly colored bandanna and tie it to the antenna.

Tamara Johnson, Memphis, Tenn.

MATCH GAME We rented a car last summer to tour northern Italy. Initially, we contacted Europcar (europcar.com) and got a quote of more than $500. We then clicked on a rental-car link from Best Fares (bestfares.com) and received an offer that knocked off about $50. When we mentioned to Europcar that we'd seen lower offers on the Web, they told us that if we sent them the URL and they could verify the offer, they'd match it. We eventually found a car that was an additional $100 cheaper from a British company. Europcar—which offered better service for our itinerary—accepted that lower price, saving us $150.

Marcia Meyer, Randallstown, Md.

ROADSIDE ASSISTANCE My husband and I travel to out-of-the-way towns where rural roads can be hard to navigate. We use a handheld GPS (Global Positioning System) to mark the spot where we're staying, the main highway turnoffs, and, most important, the turns to unmarked side roads. When we're back-tracking and arrive again at confusing intersections, we whip out our GPS and immediately know which route to take home.

Florence McGinn, Flemington, N.J.

EARLY WARNING You won't always save by bringing the rental car back early. Alamo has an early-return policy at all of its locations, designed to discourage customers from returning cars early. If you show up at the lot a day or two ahead of schedule, Alamo will recalculate what you owe them at the daily rate; if it turns out to be less than what you would have paid for the week, they'll charge a $15 fee. Yet another reason to read the fine print on your contract carefully!

Beth Ann Finster, Detroit, Mich.

BREAK THE CODE When booking a rental car online, click on "special offers" or "hot deals" to find the company's current promotional codes. Price your reservation using each code. Also, keep in mind that rates fluctuate according to seasons and slow periods. I managed to save more than $170 on a ten-day rental in Orlando, Fla., by changing my reservation dates twice and by using different codes.

Jeff Thomsen, Lenexa, Kans.

WHEN IN ROMA Get the right maps. For road trips on the Continent, European maps are much more helpful when it comes to reading road signs. They'll say Napoli instead of Naples, Firenze rather than Florence. I could spend all day waiting for a road sign for Munich and miss the exit for München.

Cynthia Stone Stewart, Dallas, Tex.

ROAD TEST Don't rush off the car-rental lot. Before driving away—especially in foreign countries where the controls might be unfamiliar—test the headlights and brakes, and look for the extra tire and changing tools. I once had a rental with malfunctioning brakes in Mexico and caused a minor accident—one that could certainly have been avoided had I checked them properly before leaving the lot.

Doreen Stelton, Lemont, Ill.

ON THE UP-AND-UP When parking in a crowded garage, don't settle for the first space available on a lower level. It's probably a half-day hike from the elevator. Instead, drive to the upper levels, where you can usually park right next to the elevator. This tip was very useful in Las Vegas, especially when checking in and out of hotels with our luggage.

Shane Kays, Jacksonville, Ill.

FOLLOW THE LEADER Driving around Italy last summer, my husband and I found that even the most detailed maps left us scratching our heads in confusion. Desperate and lost, we decided to follow a tour bus. Guess what? It got us exactly where we wanted to go.

Cindy Marcus, Valencia, Calif.

MIND THE CAP The last time we were in England, I met another American at the car-rental agency. He had just returned his rental and was annoyed he had to pay for a missing hubcap. He said that between negotiating the narrow roads, having the steering wheel on the right side of the car, and driving on the left side of the road, he couldn't judge exactly where the left front wheel was. As a result, he repeatedly hit the curb, eventually knocking off a hubcap. Later that trip, while visiting Hadrian's Wall, I noticed many cars in the parking lot were missing hubcaps. I'm glad I had put my left front hubcap in the trunk.

Bernard Hershkowitz, Commack, N.Y.

LIMO SCENE To party like a rock star in New York, negotiate with one of the many limousine drivers that park outside the clubs and bars in SoHo and the Meatpacking District. Tell them you'd like a one-hour city tour before being dropped off at your hotel. As a group of five, we tried this recently and paid $25 each for the special treatment! It was a marvelous way to see the city after dark.

Jules R. Cattie III, Colts Neck, N.J.

ONLINE OPPORTUNITY At London's Heathrow airport, we tried to rent a car without a reservation, but Enterprise said it was sold out. So we went to the Avis counter next door and were quoted a rate of $381 for a three-day rental. We then found an Internet kiosk at the airport and logged on to Expedia, where we booked an Enterprise car for $30 a day—a savings of more than 300 percent! When we went back to the Enterprise desk with our reservation in hand, a car was ready for us.

Mirvet Sidhom, Brossard, Que.

BIN THERE, DONE THAT I take each of my grandchildren on a road trip the summer each turns twelve. The trips range in length from two weeks to a month and require careful packing. I've learned to put our clothes and any snack items we'll need in large plastic bins that fit in the back of my minivan. We each bring a small bag and pack it every evening with items we'll need for that night and the next day: no lugging heavy suitcases in and out of motels or hotels.

Patsy Maddox, Fairfax, Va.

RAINY-DAY PLAN Whenever I know I'll be renting a car, I pack a couple of folded paper towels and two small spray bottles—one filled with window cleaner and the other with Rain-X, a product that repels raindrops. It's hard enough driving an unfamiliar car in an unfamiliar location. At least with a clean windshield I'm able to see properly, no matter the weather.

Ed Rainer, Lanoka Harbor, N.J.

GOT IT COVERED? With two of our last three car rentals, the local branch wanted documentation beyond the standard insurance card issued by our insurance company. In San Juan, we were delayed a half hour while the agent made phone calls to verify that our liability insurance was good in Puerto Rico. In Miami, if we hadn't provided proof that our insurance covered rental cars, we would've been charged a daily collision insurance fee. Fortunately, we knew ahead of time and took a copy of the pertinent section of our policy. Our credit card included car rental insurance, but proof of that coverage was also required.

Carole Goodyear, Niceville, Fla.

THINK TANK I always take a digital picture of the gas gauge to prove that I returned the rental car with a full tank. Some agencies try to charge for a minimal amount of gas when they "top off" the tank (which you're not supposed to do anyway). I've used these digital photographs to get refunds for gas charges that appeared on my credit-card bill after the fact.

Jeff Mishur, Roselle, Ill.

VALET VOUS? Rather than automatically using your hotel's valet parking, you should check to see if there's an adjacent parking lot or garage that offers a better rate. On a recent trip, I was able to park across the street from my hotel for $10 per day—versus $27 per day to valet park with the hotel.

Charles LaFleur, Baton Rouge, La.

CAMERA READY In Europe, my husband and I like to use public transportation. As a result, we frequently find ourselves studying itineraries displayed on train station walls, trying to read schedules posted at bus stops, or staring at kiosk-size town maps. On our last trip, my husband snapped digital photographs of those things. We were able to take the map or itinerary with us and could refer to it as needed by using the zoom feature.

Anne Supsic, St. Leonard, Md.

MARK THE SPOTS < < < < < < < < < < < <

I prefer laminated city maps because I can circle all the things I want to see in a given day with a dark erasable marker. Once I have everything marked, I plan my route and start walking. The next day, I erase the previous day's marks and begin all over again.

Sandy Hughes, Smyrna, Ga.

CHANGE IS GOOD Carry the exact change for public transportation. In Venice, we were annoyed when a vaporetto (water taxi) ticket-taker refused to give us our change. Later, we discovered that if you don't have the exact fare, ticket agents make no promises about giving change.

Dana Hunting, Seattle, Wash.

WALK LIKE AN EGYPTIAN In Cairo, taxi fares are higher if you leave from a hotel. To save money, walk to the nearest main street. Never agree to pay more than 10 pounds (less than $2) for a ride within the downtown area. Trips to the pyramids in Giza or to Khan el-Khalili cost a bit more.

Daniel Zeytoonian, Fayetteville, N.C.

STRIKE UP A CONVERSATION If you visit a country where you don't speak the language, pick up a book of your hotel's matches or one of its business cards; they usually have the hotel's name and address printed on them. Then when you're out sightseeing and want to return to your hotel, show the matchbook or card to the cabdriver if he doesn't speak English.

Verne F. Noyes, Silver Spring, Md.

UN-FARE? Before traveling by taxi in foreign (or even domestic) locations, ask a local (perhaps stopping in shops to question the sales staff) what the approximate taxi fare would be to a particular location. They've always been pleased to help me. In this manner, I can avoid paying the inflated tourist rates!

Carol P. McCrea, Redmond, Ore.

MOBILE HOMING Tell me I'm not alone: Almost every time I park my car at the airport, I have trouble finding it when I return. (I even reported my car stolen once after searching for hours, only to discover I was in the wrong lot!) I now use my cell phone to leave myself a message as to where I've parked my car.

Perry Babel, Lakewood, Colo.

JUMBO SAVINGS Going farther into China from Hong Kong? Rather than flying from Hong Kong International, consider departing from Guangzhou or Shenzhen. You can save 40 to 60 percent on airfare—more than enough to pay for the TurboJet ferry from Hong Kong to Shenzhen (from $26) or the slightly less convenient express train from Hong Kong's Hung Hom station to Guangzhou (about $30). There's a free shuttle bus from the ferry terminal to Shenzhen airport, but you'll have to take a taxi to Guangzhou Baiyun airport from the Guangzhou Dong (East) train station.

George Lindamood, Sequim, Wash.

TRAIN OF THOUGHT My husband and I always travel around Europe by train. When we arrive in any city, we first stop at a ticket window and get all the information we'll need for the next leg of our journey. This gives us plenty of time to find an English-speaking ticket agent who'll print out departure times and platform numbers for us. Before leaving the station, we can note the location of the platform we'll be looking for that morning. One wrong move when you're rushing for a train and you could end up in the wrong city!

Betty Lynn, Overland Park, Kans.

WATER LINE A water bus runs along the Intracoastal Waterway in Fort Lauderdale. You can get on and off wherever and as often as you'd like for $10 a day, and the stops give you easy access to many hotels, shops, and restaurants (watertaxi.com/ftlaud).

Erna Mattiace, Philadelphia, Pa.

RING ROAD You'd be wise to heed the unspoken rule of always traveling counterclockwise on Ireland's Ring of Kerry. Roads are narrow, with occasional steep drops on the outside. When two cars pass each other, going in opposite directions, the resulting do-si-do can be hair-raising. If you're truly unlucky and meet a tour bus at a narrow pass, you may have to back up until you reach a place where the less maneuverable vehicle can make its way around you.

Geanie Roake, South Jordan, Utah

BETTER BUS To travel between Santiago and other parts of Chile, consider using Tur-Bus (turbus.com). In the *salón cama* class, the seats fully recline and Spanish-language movies are available. A one-way overnight ticket from Santiago to the city of Puerto Montt starts at $40—much less expensive than a plane ticket and a night in a hotel.

Susan Mead, Portland, Ore.

SHOW THE WAY Finding anything in Tokyo is difficult when you don't speak Japanese, so here's what I suggest: Buy postcards of the places you want to see; an English description of the landmark is usually found on the back. Show the postcard to a taxi driver, and he'll take you to the spot.

Jim Dinsmore, Northridge, Calif.

BERMUDA SHORTCUT In Bermuda, a $28 tourist pass buys three days of unlimited bus travel around the island. This includes service to a multitude of beautiful beaches and unlimited ferry service (the ferries are a great way to tour the inner harbor).

Carolyn and Dave Holland, Hicksville, N.Y.

CARD CARRYING Transport for London sells its Travelcards at ticket-on-line.com and charges nothing to mail them to you before you leave home. Cards are good for three or seven days of unlimited travel on the Tube (subway), light-rail system, and buses. Most tourist sites are located in zones one and two; a seven-day card for these zones costs only $41. With individual trips costing approximately $5.50, the card pays for itself in less than two trips per day.

Jeanette Langdell, Sunnyvale, Calif.

A RAIL BARGAIN Before my husband and I traveled to Japan, we found out that if we purchased a Japan Rail Pass (available at japanrailpass.net) in the United States, it would cost a fraction of what we'd spend on the individual tickets in Japan. Since the country can be so expensive, the savings were a tremendous help to our budget.

Pearle Herndon, Mount Dora, Fla.

PASS PERKS Read the fine print on your rail pass. You can often use it to save money on other modes of public transportation. With a Scandinavian rail pass, for example, you'll pay less to ride the ferries. In Switzerland, a rail pass can get you free bus rides, as well as complimentary entrance to museums and discounts on funiculars and hotel accommodations.

Jessica Lees, West Chester, Pa.

BIKES ON BOARD We decided to take our bikes on our last Caribbean cruise. It was a little crowded in the cabin, so the steward let us store them down the hall with the wheelchairs. We were last off the ship when we docked in Bermuda, but after five minutes we'd left our fellow passengers in the dust. And in less than fifteen minutes, we were far away from the busy port, enjoying a beautiful, deserted snorkeling beach.

Wayne Matchett, Chesapeake, Va.

A MAN WITH A VAN When I'm on a cruise with my wife's family and we're in a foreign city for the day, I get off the boat as soon as we dock and hail a taxi. I ask the driver to call his dispatcher and find me a van with an English-speaking driver. Then I negotiate an hourly rate and a pickup time at the dock. The family tours together for a few hours, and then each couple either gets dropped off where they want to spend extra time or returns to the boat (this is great for my elderly in-laws). We get a tailor-made city tour for a much cheaper rate than if we had booked through the cruise line.

Stuart Hanzman, Alpharetta, Ga.

TRANSPORT AUTHORITY For the most comprehensive information regarding travel by train or by ship, check out seat61.com. I've found that the site has all sorts of helpful advice for Africa, Asia, Europe, and the Middle East.

Kay Bozich Owens, Middletown, N.C.

CHAPTER SEVEN

<BT<<<<<<<<<<<<<<<<<<<<<<<<<<<<<<<<<<<<<<<<<<
9781594741777<<<<<<<<<<<<<<<<<<<<<<<<<<<<07

MEGA ZIPLOC Ziploc now makes extra-large bags with handles. They're nearly two feet by two feet, and although Ziploc advertises them as being good for storage, they're also useful for traveling. Bring one on long shopping excursions and then use it as an extra carry-on for souvenirs on the way home.

Meredith McCulloch, Bedford, Mass.

MAIL BOX Sending a flat-rate Priority Mail box costs $8.10, no matter how much it weighs or which state it's going to. After accumulating too much stuff to fit in my suitcase during a trip to Atlanta, I filled a box with laundry, souvenirs, and gifts for my grandchildren, and mailed it to my home address.

Eleanor Waterhouse, Kailua, Hawaii

YE OLDE POSTCARD Anyone tired of the same boring postcards that are found at every roadside tourist trap should try shopping for vintage postcards at an antiques shop. They're a great addition to any photo album, as they often show what the local attractions looked like prior to development.

Christian Galloway, Leesburg, Va.

HAGGLE HELP Consider asking your driver or tour guide to haggle on your behalf at bazaars and souks. (But don't let them lead you to places where they might have a connection to the shopkeeper.) The money you tip them will usually be less than the markup on prices for tourists.

Rami Aboumahadi, Boynton Beach, Fla.

SEE WHAT'S IN STORE If you plan to buy crafts in a country where bargaining is expected, use the time it takes for luggage to be unloaded to scope out the airport stores. Jot down items you like and their retail prices. If you find a similar item while touring the country, you have a top-end bargaining point. If you don't find the object at a better price, you can always pick it up at the airport while you're waiting for your flight home.

Deborah Seter, Punta Gorda, Fla.

BUYERS AND CELLARS Check out grocery stores in Europe for bargains on wine. On our last trip to Italy, I found a 1993 Banfi Brunello in a small market for $16. If I could find it at all in my local wine shop, that same bottle would cost more than $100. I only wish I had listened to my husband and bought all three of the bottles the store had.

Stacy Shaw, Chicago, Ill.

WOMAN OF THE CLOTH On a trip to Nice I fell in love with the wonderful Provençal tablecloths and napkins, but they were very expensive. So I found the word for fabric (*tissu*) in my English-French dictionary and used the phone book to locate stores in the area. I came home with yards of beautiful fabrics and made the tablecloths and napkins myself.

Laurel Swan, Bloomfield, Conn.

SUPERMARKET SOUVENIRS Easily packable, local specialty foods make great gifts for family and friends at home. At the huge Safeway in Kihei, Maui, we found a great selection of chocolate-covered macadamia nuts and Kona coffee beans in elegant gift boxes for far cheaper than in tourist-oriented shops. European grocery stores abound with gift ideas: British teas, French mustards and vinegars, and Italian olive oils are just a few examples. Just bear in mind that meats, produce, and other fresh items are a customs no-no.

Jennifer Beach, Alexandria, Va.

FASHION FORWARD When my husband and I visit places like India or Thailand, we pack only one extra change of clothes. When we arrive, we hit a local market and buy local attire—woven shirts, saris, sarongs, etc. Not only does this make packing easier, but we get a better cultural experience and end up with lots of wearable souvenirs!

Alice Fraser, Port Townsend, Wash.

DON'T MESS WITH TAXES Don't be too quick to grab one of those GST tax-rebate envelopes that are everywhere in Canadian airports. The envelopes look official, but they're really from companies that process the request for you and often pocket 15 percent or more. Instead, go to the Canada Revenue Agency Web site (cra-arc.gc.ca), download the Application for Visitor Tax Refund, and then file the request yourself. Your check will arrive in a few weeks. Just remember to get your receipt stamped by the Canada Border Services Agency at the airport.

Tony Reynolds, Berryville, Va.

NUMBER CRUNCHER It helps to have a calculator if you plan to do a lot of shopping in foreign markets. When you find something you like, hand the seller the calculator and ask him to enter his best price. It's easy to convert the response into dollars so you know what you're spending. If necessary, the calculator can be used to haggle, especially if you don't speak the language.

Becky Sapp, Arlington, Va.

BANG FOR THE BUCK While wandering in the Shihlin Night Market in Taipei, I was surprised to see the Taiwanese equivalent of a 99-cent store. It was full of fun gifts for kids and our more easily amused friends. We picked up a couple of cool kitchen items that would have cost at least $10 each back home!

Mark Yim, Los Angeles, Calif.

LAST FOR THE LEAST We like to buy shipboard souvenirs, so we try to choose a ship that's completing its run of an area—that's when merchandise is generally put on sale. Last year, for example, on a sailing in South America, all of the T-shirts, glassware, and rain jackets were 75 percent off.

Carol Callahan, Mechanicsville, Va.

K-MARVELOUS When you're shopping for alcohol on any Caribbean island, ask if there's a Kmart nearby. Often the discounter is a short distance from the docks where the cruise ships tie up and has an extensive selection at prices lower than the liquor stores on the main drag. While you're there, pick up that extra roll of film or the sunscreen you forgot.

Andrea Mansfield, Hamilton Square, N.J.

SNACK ATTACK As you leave Kahului Airport on Maui, you'll pass both Kmart and Wal-Mart. Stop in and stock up on snacks, sodas, beer, wine, etc., to bring to your hotel. We did, and this allowed us to sit by the pool and indulge without paying outrageous minibar prices.

Aaron Thompson, Bel Air, Md.

ON THE MENU By the time I got home from my first trip to Europe in 1963, I'd collected menus from several restaurants I liked. I threw them into a box. In 1988, I returned to Europe and went to the Middle East. Once again, I picked up a few menus. This time I had them all framed and they now hang in my kitchen. Since then, I've added to the collection. It's fun looking at the prices and remembering the good times—plus they make great conversation pieces when I have a party.

Jerri Moore, Atlanta, Ga.

SINGLE SERVING If you're traveling solo and want some company for dinner, try the sushi bar at a Japanese restaurant. It's a great place to meet locals. Plus, you'll receive extra attention and special recommendations from the chef.

Marcie Rubenstein, Montreal, Que.

FINE CHINESE In North American cities with large Chinese communities, choose a family-run Chinese restaurant and ask for the set family meals, usually written in Chinese. They are more authentic than those typically offered to tourists and people who are not Chinese—not to mention a better value. In San Francisco, for example, you can enjoy a five-course meal, which easily feeds a family of four, for less than $20.

Winston Wong, San Francisco, Calif.

MENUS THAT DELIVER < < < < < < < <

I carry bilingual takeout menus when traveling to countries like China, Korea, and Vietnam. When I'm at a restaurant with no menu (or one that I can't read), I give mine to the waiter so he can point to dishes they can prepare. I've learned to pack a few extra menus, as the restaurants often like to keep a copy.

Charles Locher, Richmond, Calif.

EASY AS PIE To feed a family of four in a very expensive tropical location like Anguilla or Bermuda (or most other Caribbean locations, for that matter), check to see if your hotel has phone books and look up the local pizza place. Nine times out of ten the pizza purveyors will deliver for free. You'll end up spending no more than $20 on pizza, bread sticks, and soda.

Bianca Mims, Houston, Tex.

CHEAP EATS Using restaurant.com, you can buy gift certificates good at eateries in your destination city, regularly snagging (in my experience) $25 certificates for as little as $5 to $8. The site is awesome, and it works as well for restaurant certificates in your own city and for obtaining gifts for friends.

Derrick Tennant, Atlanta, Ga.

UNCORK THE SAVINGS We recently discovered that some owners of small family-run hotels in Italy will let you BYOB to meals. On a trip with friends to Pescasseroli in the beautiful Abruzzi Mountains, we spent a long weekend at the Hotel Valle dell'Oro. Room rates included all meals, but didn't cover any alcoholic beverages. Since there were six of us, bringing store-bought wine to dinner each night saved us a lot.

Maria Pipolo Eberlin, Naples, Italy

WILL WORK FOR FOOD While traveling abroad, I've frequently encountered some appallingly bad (and often very funny) English translations of menus. In those cases, I simply offered to clean up the translations in exchange for a meal. This has worked quite a few times.

William Boyle, Washington, D.C.

STORED FOOD While traveling in Japan with our six children this summer, my wife and I discovered a way to cut down on our lunch and dinner expenses. Almost every department store offers a selection of precooked meals that the Japanese buy and take home to eat. The food was wonderful, our children could choose things that interested them, and the experience was purely Japanese. The food emporiums, usually found in the basement, should not be confused with the expensive restaurants that most department stores have on their top floors.

Ralph Ellsworth, San Juan Capistrano, Calif.

COUNTER INTUITIVE Deli counters in grocery stores are great mealtime alternatives to restaurants or fast-food fare when you're exploring the United States. The food is fresh, there's a big variety (hot and cold), and economically, it's a great break. I recently had a complete hot meal, including beverage, for $3 from a grocery-store deli.

Teresa G. Barcus, St. Paul, Minn.

MAKING A POINT Going to a place where you don't speak the language? Take along a picture booklet filled with examples of common food items (chicken, cow, rice, bottled water, coffee, wine, etc.) and use it to find dishes you like—you only have to point to the picture of what you want. We did this during a recent trip to Asia and always had wonderful meals.

Mario Gonzalez, Laredo, Tex.

BAHAMIAN RHAPSODY Dining out on Paradise Island, in the Bahamas, is very expensive, especially at the resorts. But if you walk over the bridge between Paradise Island and New Providence Island, you'll find a group of food stands owned by locals. At MacKenzie's, for example, a dinner of fried breaded conch, peas, rice, and fried plantains is $8. Wash it down with a $3 Kalik beer. The bridge is a little steep, but the view of the harbor, including the many cruise ships and local fishing boats, is terrific.

Dawn O'Leary, O'Fallon, Ill.

SPICE IT UP If you know you'll be cooking while on vacation, bring along small amounts of the spices you need for your favorite recipes. You'll save by not buying large containers of spices.

Joan Phillips, Golden, Colo.

STANDING ORDER When having the traditional breakfast of cappuccino and a sweet roll at a local café in Italy, you will note that the natives always have their breakfast while standing. That's because the cost of a stand-up breakfast for two is around $6, while the exact same breakfast served at a table a few feet away from the bar is closer to $19.

Steve Szalewicz, Sharon, Conn.

IN A JIF Always carry peanut butter. A plastic jar is easy to pack, doesn't need refrigeration, is a great source of protein, and makes a quick, cheap meal when coupled with local bread. (But don't forget to pack a plastic knife for spreading it.)

Nancy Norman, Lancaster, N.Y.

CROWD PLEASERS If you're looking for authentic street food—whether you're in New York or Bangkok—don't buy from the pitifully lonely vendor who has no customers. Head to the cart with the longest line of hungry people in front of it. Locals know which vendors serve the best (and safest) food. Even if you have to wait, your stomach will thank you.

Bryan Thao Worra, St. Paul, Minn.

BOWLED OVER A company called Orikaso makes brightly colored polypropylene sheets that can be folded—kind of like origami—to form a dish, bowl, or cup. The sheets are lightweight and reusable, and you simply flatten them when you're finished. We found ours at a sporting goods store, but you can also buy them online. Check orikaso.com for retailers.

Susan Day, Brooklyn Park, Minn.

WHAT'S COOKING I carry recipe cards with me to jot down interesting dishes I come across while on vacation. (I also like to use colorful postcards from the area I'm visiting and trim them to fit my recipe box.) Here's a wonderful dessert idea I brought home after spending a rainy afternoon with my husband in a London pub: Top a warm waffle with vanilla ice cream, maple syrup, and chopped pecans. It's heaven with a cup of hot tea.

Susan Mullens, Scottsdale, Ariz.

CHAPTER EIGHT

BUDGET TRAVEL

8. 186-213

OUT AND ABOUT

VISITING AND SIGHTSEEING

<BT<<<<<<<<<<<<<<<<<<<<<<<<<<<<<<<<<<
9781594741777<<<<<<<<<<<<<<<<<<<<07

SEIZE THE DAY Don't save the best for the last day. If you wait until the end of your trip for "must-do" activities, you won't be able to reschedule if something unforeseen happens. I planned a snorkeling excursion for my final day in San Diego, but the waters were too rough, and the trip had to be canceled.

Melissa Coplak, Astoria, N.Y.

TAKE IT AS A SIGN I always snap photographs of scenic-highway markers, park-entrance signs, and the like. These informational photos are put into our album to help identify the many sites that we visited.

Betty L. Cox, Flagler Beach, Fla.

MEMBERSHIP HAS ITS PRIVILEGES If your travels take you to U.S. cities large enough to have museums, zoos, and/or botanical gardens, consider buying a membership in your home city's counterpart. Many have reciprocal privileges with institutions elsewhere. A membership at Chicago's Lincoln Park Zoo, for example, lets you see the National Zoo in Washington, D.C., and zoos in Los Angeles, Des Moines, and Jackson, Mississippi, at no charge.

Alice M. Solovy, Skokie, Ill.

MEMORIAL DAYS Visitors to Prague who want to see the Jewish Holocaust memorials should remember that synagogues close early on Fridays and stay closed on Saturdays. Make sure you aren't there only for the weekend.

Joanne Steuer, Los Angeles, Calif.

PARIS SCOPED When in Paris, make sure you pick up a copy of *Pariscope* at a local newsstand. It's a cheap little guide that'll clue you in to all the cultural events going on that week. There's an English-language section, too.

Mary Cheely, Chicago, Ill.

PASS GO Paris offers a remarkable pass that every tourist should obtain. The Carte Orange (from $20) allows unlimited use of the Métro for an entire week (a much better deal than another card developed for tourists). Get the Carte Orange at Métro ticket windows by saying, "Une Carte Orange, hebdomadaire, s'il vous plait."

Jessica Lees, West Chester, Pa.

A LITTLE DAY MUSIC On Wednesdays at 12:30 in the afternoon, the world-renowned Amsterdam Sinfonietta orchestra holds rehearsals that are free and open to the public (check at concertgebouw.nl). Relaxing in the historic concert hall—built in 1888—is a wonderful way to take a break from sightseeing. The locals start lining up around noon, but we were able to get good seats just minutes before the show started.

Janet Barton, Sausalito, Calif.

ZOO KEEPER You'll spend $60.50 per adult to visit both the San Diego Zoo and Wild Animal Park. But for $99, an annual membership grants two adults from the same household unlimited admission to both parks for a year, unlimited use of the Skyfari aerial tram, two guest passes (more than $50 in value), four discount guest coupons ($20 value), four two-for-one zoo bus-tour coupons, and more. To top it all off, most of the $99 is tax-deductible! Apply at sandiegozoo.org or at the park.

Dorinda Won, Honolulu, Hawaii

ASK QUESTIONS FIRST, SHOOT LATER Photographs can't be taken within most tombs at the Valley of Kings and the Valley of Queens in Egypt. I saw guards confiscate rolls of film and memory cards from digital cameras (they won't let you just erase the images). As with everywhere else, it's best to ask before pulling out your camera in historic or religious places.

Samantha Reguieg, West Hills, Calif.

OZ FEST The three-day See Sydney & Beyond Smartvisit Card (seesydneycard.com) grants you admission to more than forty attractions in Sydney and the Blue Mountains. It includes unlimited rides on CityRail, buses, light-rail trains, and all ferries except the Manly JetCat. The card easily pays for itself.

Mandy Sutyak, Niwot, Colo.

COLOSSAL IDEA Even in the off-season, the lines to purchase tickets for Rome's Colosseum can be more than an hour long. Rather than wait with everyone else, our guide took us to a ticket window at the Palatine Museum, a five-minute walk away (Via di San Gregorio 30). He explained that admission to the Palatine also covers the Colosseum, for the same $15. We walked back to the Colosseum, past a line 100 yards long, flashed our Palatine tickets, and got right in.

Gary Minjock, Seven Hills, Ohio

FRENCH BLISS Buy the Paris Museum Pass (parismuseumpass.fr) at participating museums before heading to popular sights like Versailles and the Louvre. You'll get a day of unlimited access to more than sixty top attractions in and around Paris—and you'll be able to skip long lines at the entrances. It costs $38 for two days.

Mike McDole, Chicago, Ill.

ANIMAL ATTRACTION If you plan to spend more than five days in Kruger or any of the other nineteen national parks in South Africa, you can save a lot of money by obtaining a Wild Card (sanparks.org). It costs $114 for one person or $199 for two and offers unlimited access to the parks for a year. Standard entrance fees at Kruger are $17 per person per day.

Glen Kirkpatrick, Molalla, Ore.

CANADIAN BECKON Look for the Montreal Museum Pass, which allows use of the city's transit system plus entrance to thirty-two of Montreal's most popular attractions for three consecutive days. It costs $39 at the participating museums and attractions, as well as at the three tourist information booths in town (174 Notre-Dame St. East; 1255 Peel St., Suite 100; and 576 Ste-Catherine East).

David R. Cohen, Lake Worth, Fla.

DRAMATIC DISCOUNT If you're in Sydney, give your wallet a break and, instead of the opera, catch a play at the National Institute of Dramatic Art (nida.edu.au). For $21, you can watch future Nicole Kidmans and Russell Crowes perfect their craft at the country's premier drama school.

Colleen Haskell, Santa Monica, Calif.

CINEMA PARADISE On Saturdays, the Los Angeles Conservancy (laconservancy.org) leads $10 walking tours of downtown L.A.'s old movie palaces. See where Charlie Chaplin's *City Lights* premiered, the Orpheum Theater, and many other spectacularly preserved theaters along Broadway. A map for a self-guided tour is posted on the Web site.

Susan Matheson, Los Angeles, Calif.

COOL BUS Most hotels in Cancún have tour-operator desks selling day trips to archaeological sites such as Chichén Itzá and Tulúm. Instead of shelling out big bucks, take a local bus (60¢) to the downtown station and buy a round-trip bus ticket for a quarter of the prepackaged-tour price. The buses are air-conditioned and allow you to explore at your own pace. You can also arrive way ahead of the crowd, during the cooler part of the day.

Lolly Pineda, Millbrae, Calif.

QUID YOU NOT I discovered a great Web site while my family and I were living in London: londonfreelist.com. It lists events and attractions around the city that are free (or nearly free).

Peggy Bennett, W. Hartford, Conn.

JOURNAL JUMPSTART Before we went to London, I created a personalized booklet on our computer with fill-in pages like "the new foods I tried were," "best candy," "words I learned," and "most fun/boring museums." My daughter, who might have been daunted by lots of blank journal pages, had a blast answering the questions and filling in all the details.

Mary Cronin, Harwich, Mass.

FREE QUARTER Instead of paying for a tour of New Orleans' French Quarter, join a free, ranger-led walking tour provided by the National Park Service. The one-mile walks depart from the NPS Visitor Center at 9:30 a.m. daily. Arrive early, because the tours are limited to twenty-five people.

Kirk Miller, Richardson, Tex.

TAKE MANHATTAN Every Thursday and Saturday at noon, the Downtown Alliance (downtownny.com) has free 90-minute walking tours of downtown New York, including the U.S. Custom House and the New York Stock Exchange.

Bill Wang, San Francisco, Calif.

TOUR DE FRANCE If you want to see a show in Paris—say, at the Moulin Rouge—consider booking through a tour-bus company like Cityrama or France Tourisme. You'll receive discounted admission, transportation to the show, and an additional tour that night (a Seine River cruise or "Illuminations," for example). We paid $90 per person for an entire evening of entertainment as opposed to $122 each for the show tickets alone.

Lori Swerda, Brunswick, Md.

ANCIENT IRELAND Admission to many of Ireland's historical sites can be costly. Instead, buy the Heritage Card, good for unlimited admission for one year to more than seventy heritage sites across the country (including Dublin and Kilkenny castles). The card costs $26 for adults, $21 for seniors, $10 for students and children, or $69 for families. Buy them at the heritage sites or at heritageireland.ie.

Nuala Barner, Westwood, Mass.

ART APPRECIATION Want to visit museums with your children without the boredom and tears? Go to the gift shop first and buy postcards of the museum's most famous works. Have your kids treasure hunt for these masterpieces. When you get home the postcards can go right into your trip album.

Daphna Woolfe, San Jose, Calif.

SEAT SAVER Looking for Broadway discounts? As an alternative to the TKTS booths, where you could spend half the day waiting in line, check out broadwaybox.com. This site gives discount codes that result in up to 50 percent off box-office prices. I got $55 tickets for *Rent* (they're usually $95), and the seats were in the orchestra section.

Grace Bulanan, Daly City, Calif.

FAR SIGHTED To avoid walking around gawking at skyscrapers while sightseeing in cities like New York, I pack a small pair of binoculars. When I spot an interesting building, I step out of the flow of traffic on the sidewalk, back up to a wall, and enjoy the architectural details or read inscriptions.

Virgina Hendley, Rio Rancho, N.M.

TREKS MEX Visit México Desconocido for information ranging from pre-Columbian history to suggested day-to-day itineraries (mexicodesconocido.com/english). Designed to promote the historical, cultural, and natural wealth of Mexico, the site lists packages sorted by interest, region, and theme. You can choose to book services offered by the site's partners or use the information to develop your own itinerary.

Carlos J. Martínez, Houston, Tex.

POLITICAL ADVANTAGE If you're planning to spend time in Washington, D.C., always write in advance to your state's congressional representatives, requesting free maps, brochures, tickets to attend sessions of Congress, and even discounted tour tickets.

J. Morrill, Alexandria, Va.

FERRY HELPFUL In Hong Kong, stop by the tourist office at the airport's arrivals area. Free tickets are available for Thursday and Saturday cruises on a restored Chinese junk that departs from Kowloon Public Pier. Space is limited and seats fill up fast, so reserve in person (and remember to bring your passport) as soon as you arrive in Hong Kong!

Melody Ryan, Lexington, Ky.

BICYCLES BUILT FOR TOURS A bike tour will offer a good introduction to a place, and you'll cover much more ground than if you were on foot. In Buenos Aires, for example, Lan & Kramer Bike Tours (biketours.com.ar) has a few guided itineraries that are fun for all ages and abilities.

Meda Florin, Carmichael, Calif.

CYCLICAL THINKING We're active travelers but find guided bike tours from companies like Backroads too expensive. Our advice: After rolling into town, ask at a bike shop for the best routes. Better yet, call or e-mail before you leave home (search the Web). We've found group rides and races this way, and have made a lot of friends. We're instant locals!

Glenn and Michelle Schultes, Anchorage, Alaska

GET THE RUNDOWN When I travel to a new city, I check with the local running club to see if there are any events planned during my stay. The entry fee is usually donated to a charity, and I get great exercise, meet locals, and tour a part of the city I may not have known about.

Kelly Christiansen, Ocoee, Fla.

A LIFT FOR LESS The next time you ski Summit County, Colorado, buy your lift tickets in Denver instead of waiting until you get to the resorts. Discounted tickets for Breckenridge, Keystone, Arapahoe Basin, Copper Mountain, and others are sold at grocery stores and sports shops. We like Colorado Ski & Golf and King Soopers.

Wendy Kunze, Clinton Township, Mich.

SKI RING Spring skiing often means a wild temperature shift from morning to afternoon. If you want the option of removing outer layers or switching to a lighter ski jacket midday, attach the lift ticket to your clothing with a split-ring key ring. You'll be able to move your ticket as the weather warms up.

Don Harbold, Traverse City, Mich.

SCUBA LIBRE Certified scuba divers who take prescription medications should keep a doctor's permission-to-dive statement with their certification cards. On a recent trip to Jamaica, I truthfully completed a lengthy questionnaire about my health, revealing that I have medically controlled high blood pressure and cholesterol. I was told I could not dive without a doctor's OK, even though I exercise regularly, am very fit, and have no other health issues. I now carry a letter from my doctor attesting to my fitness for scuba diving.

Ginny Ganthner, Reno, Nev.

THERE'S THE RUB I've discovered a wonderful way to enjoy massages at a fraction of the usual cost. Some massage-training schools provide superb service in a spa-type environment. Do a Google search to see if there are training programs near your next vacation destination.

Karen Gardiner, Alexandria, Va.

GO TAKE A BIKE For a 20-kroner deposit (about $3.50), visitors to Copenhagen, Denmark, can borrow a bicycle at one of 110 different locations throughout the city and explore the sights at their own speed (bycyklen.dk). Return the bike to any of these racks, and your deposit is refunded.

Gunhild McKinney, Detroit, Mich.

COURSE LANGUAGE Before heading to the Phoenix area, visit arizonagolfer.net for discounts on last-minute greens fees. I've seen savings as high as 80 percent.

Bev Marshall, Bellingham, Wash.

LEI OF THE LAND Visit calendar.gohawaii.com for a calendar of events in Hawaii. My husband and I joined a terrific (free) guided hike on Kauai—we wouldn't have known about it had we not checked the Web site.

Gina Kelly, Fort Collins, Colo.

PERSONALIZED POSTCARDS Create your own postcards by writing on the back of photographs that you've taken and developed while still on your trip.

Connie Van Brocklin, St. Augustine, Fla.

DOUBLE EXPOSURE I travel with two cameras: a digital SLR for the majority of my shots, and a small disposable camera for when I ask strangers to take pictures of me. As much as I tend to trust other people, I'm not ready to hand over my $1,000 camera to someone I don't know at all.

Sam Antonio, San Diego, Calif.

CAPTURING A MOOD I enjoy off-peak travel best—rates are cheaper, lines are shorter—but the weather can be iffy. To combat Mother Nature's unpredictability, I always pack a roll or two of black-and-white film. While dreary-day color photos bring only consoling remarks from friends, black-and-white film tends to lend a mystique to gray landscapes and creates some very dramatic Ansel Adams–esque shots.

Ed Danyo, Lancaster, Pa.

RICE AND SHINE After I fell into a stream in Cambodia, my digital camera wouldn't work. Someone suggested leaving the camera in a bag of rice overnight to draw out any condensation. By the next morning, it was dry and working perfectly.

Roger Bailey, El Dorado Hills, Calif.

MEMORY LOSS When not taking pictures, keep your memory card away from your camera. It's a simple method to ensure that any photographs you've shot will be safe even if your camera is stolen. My husband and I learned this lesson the hard way when we lost 250 shots of Kauai.

Jamie Thomas, Seattle, Wash.

DIRECT TO VIDEO My daughter and I bought disposable digital camcorders at a CVS pharmacy before going to Europe. It was a nice way to document our trip—each camera stored about 20 minutes of video. Once home, we dropped the cameras off at the pharmacy. The next day, our DVD was ready. We were very pleased with the quality and the cost: $30 for the camera and $13 for each DVD.

Maria B. Murad, Apple Valley, Minn.

CARD TRICK Accidentally reformat your camera's memory card? As long as you don't overwrite the disk by shooting more photos, those original pictures are still there. Buy another card to use in the meantime, and then, when you get home, either purchase a file-recovery software program (about $35) or take the card to a camera shop and see if someone there can help.

Julie Mancini, Dunnellon, Fla.

DATE YOURSELF Many computer photo albums use camera date stamps to organize collections. Whenever you're traveling in a time zone that might affect the date stamp (if you're crossing the International Date Line, for example), remember to reset your camera's clock.

Michael Gray, Pleasant Hill, Calif.

UNSURE SHOT Put an address label on your one-time-use camera. At a Final Four game in Indianapolis, we exchanged identical Kodak Fun Savers with another traveler so that we could take souvenir photos of each other with our respective cameras. But afterward, we couldn't tell whose camera was whose. Luckily, I remembered how many exposures remained on mine, so we got ours back. Next time, I'll just label it.

Matthew Richard, Syracuse, N.Y.

TEMPORARY LENS CAP Disposable-camera lenses scratch just like any other lens would. Place a small piece of painter's tape (or another kind that won't stick too much) over the lens to protect it from contact with other items in your purse or backpack during travel.

Hugo Scherzberg, Concord, Calif.

KEEP 'EM SEPARATED Don't put your magnetic sunglass clip-ons in the same pocket as your mass-transit fare cards or hotel key cards. I managed to erase both my subway pass and my hotel key on a recent trip.

Jim Tichenor, Buena Vista, Va.

BROLLY BAG When carrying around my small umbrella, I put it in a Ziploc bag. After using it, I can store the umbrella, back inside the Ziploc, in my shoulder bag without getting everything else soaked.

Sandy Sussman, Princeton, N.J.

DRENCHED BUT DRY If you plan to visit a theme park, always bring a few sandwich-size Ziploc bags. They'll protect your cell phone and wallet when you're riding on flumes and other water attractions.

Jack Bell, Kissimmee, Fla.

STROLL IN THE PARK At a theme park, tie a brightly colored scarf to the handle of your stroller before you enter a ride. When you return, you'll be able to quickly pick out your stroller from a sea of look-alikes.

Katrina Shelton, Beaumont, Tex.

URBAN EXPLORATION A small compass is a great travel aid. Aside from the obvious benefits during country drives or hikes, it's extremely helpful in navigating winding city streets and orienting yourself once you exit a subway station.

William Schaeffer, Fly Creek, N.Y.

CHAPTER NINE

<BT<<<<<<<<<<<<<<<<<<<<<<<<<<<<<<<<<<<<<<<<<
9781594741777<<<<<<<<<<<<<<<<<<<<<<<07

CALL LETTERS Making international calls back to the States can be confusing if you're using a calling card and you're dialing a number by its catchphrase, such as CALL ATT. Obviously, many countries don't have the English alphabet on the telephone keypad. My solution? I create my own small keypads on a computer, print them out, and attach them inside my wallet, to my passport, and to my calling cards.

Peter Morris, Vilas, N.C.

BLOG ROLLING By starting a blog for each trip (at blogger.com, among others), you can keep your friends and family up-to-date on your adventures. All you need is an Internet café to add entries and photos while you're on the road.

Alan A. Lew, Flagstaff, Ariz.

SAILORS' DELIGHT Public libraries in the ports of Alaska are a tremendous money-saver. Who wants to pay $5 a minute for Internet use from a cruise ship? During a port stop on a recent Alaska cruise, we found a city library that offered free Internet use for 15 to 30 minutes. Our only cost was a short wait in line.

Gail G. Jenkins, Kuna, Idaho

THE JOY OF TEXT If you're even slightly tech savvy and have a cell phone that will work overseas, check with your service provider about the cost of text messages. Some carriers offer free incoming text messages, and several Internet search engines (Yahoo, MSN, etc.) will send free text-message "alerts" to your phone while you're away. Prior to your trip, log on and request that weather forecasts and news updates be sent to your number daily. Even if you never use your phone for costly overseas calls, you can receive up-to-the-minute information, in English, about your hometown or cities on your itinerary.

Brian Mosteller, Chicago, Ill.

ADDRESS FOR SUCCESS Before leaving on a trip, I print the names and addresses of my friends and family onto clear mailing labels. (All standard word-processing programs have preset templates for creating address labels.) Then, I take the address-label sheets with me on vacation. Since the addresses are already saved in my computer and the mailing labels are adhesive, addressing postcards has become really easy.

Lisa Higgins, Oak Park, Ill.

CAFÉ SOCIETY In areas where the majority of people don't speak English, head to an Internet café. In our experience, they're full of friendly young people anxious to practice their English.

Christine and Duncan Orr, Midway, Utah

NOTE TO SELF While traveling, I love to send postcards to friends—and also to myself. I get the best photo postcard of the place I visited and write down what I did there as a reminder. When I get home, I tape them in my travel journals so I can flip back and forth between the photo and the reverie.

Kimberly Morgan, Lemon Grove, Calif.

ADDRESS E-BOOK Just before a trip to Spain, I e-mailed myself a list of addresses of the friends and family I might want to e-mail while away. At a cybercafé, I was able to simply cut and paste the list into the address line of a new message.

Rita Young, Perth Road, Ont.

GAME TIME < < < < < < < < < < < < < <

My husband and I befriended some locals in Provence by joining them in a game of *pétanque*. It was such a memorable experience that now we brush up on local games each time we plan to travel abroad. We've played dominoes in Spain and bocce in Italy.

Lesa Porché, San Francisco, Calif.

PREADDRESSED POSTCARDS Whenever I go somewhere, I bring a supply of postcards from my hometown. I write my name, address, and e-mail on the back, and offer a card to new friends so we can keep in touch. I also pack small souvenirs (key rings, etc.) that carry my local sports teams' logos. They make meaningful but inexpensive thank-you gifts for the small kindnesses that ease one's way during a trip.

Linda Phelps, Minneapolis, Minn.

STUCK ON YOU When traveling in the developing world, I always bring several packets of stickers to give to children. They're wonderful icebreakers.

Linda Vogel, Pomona, Calif.

TOYS FOR TOTS Before I visit poorer countries, I pop into a thrift store and pick up some toys, stuffed animals, and an old suitcase or carryall. I try to avoid toys like Easter bunnies or Santas, which could be offensive, and expensive things that might embarrass parents. The contents of my extra bag bring joy to countless kids who have never had a thing.

Ingrid Newkirk, Norfolk, Va.

FACE CARDS My husband and I create personal cards (like business cards) before we leave home. We put our name, address, phone, and e-mail address on them, as well as a picture of us. How many people have gotten home from a trip, looked at a slip of paper with a name and address, and wondered, Who is this? The picture helps link a name to a face.

Susan Fornoff, Woodway, Tex.

QUICKER STICKERS Every year, I get address labels from numerous charitable organizations. I keep them with me when traveling because it's the quickest way to provide my address to new friends, enter prize drawings at shops, sign guest books, etc. It's not only efficient, it can also help spread the word about worthwhile charities.

Carole Wilk, Little Neck, N.Y.

INSTAMATIC HAPPINESS Carry a Polaroid camera when traveling to developing countries. In Cambodia, several village children gathered around us, posed enthusiastically for pictures, and were fascinated by their images in our digital camera. We wanted to send them the pictures, but they were unable to tell us their address. Polaroids would have solved the problem!

Cynda Perun, Chicago, Ill.